the fourth trimester

Unfiltered, *honest* and *achievable* advice for every new mum in the first *twelve weeks* after birth

the fourth trimester

Amelia Lamont
THE MIDWIFE MUMMA

PENGUIN BOOKS

UK | USA | Canada | Ireland | Australia
India | New Zealand | South Africa | China

Penguin Books is part of the Penguin Random House group of companies whose addresses can be found at global.penguinrandomhouse.com

First published by Penguin Books in 2025

Copyright © Amelia Lamont 2025

The moral right of the author has been asserted.

All rights reserved. No part of this publication may be reproduced, published, performed in public or communicated to the public in any form or by any means without prior written permission from Penguin Random House Australia Pty Ltd or its authorised licensees.

This book was written by a midwife and certified sleep and lactation consultant. However, the information contained in this book is provided for general purposes only. It is not intended for and should not be relied upon as medical advice. If you are considering the information contained in this book regarding your or your child's health and wellbeing, you should first discuss this with a qualified medical, healthcare or other appropriate professional.

Cover design by Christabella Designs © Penguin Random House Australia Pty Ltd
Author photograph by Heather Robbins
Internal design by Post Pre-press, Australia
Typeset in 13/18 pt Birka LT Pro by Post Pre-press, Australia

Printed and bound in Australia by Griffin Press, an accredited ISO AS/NZS 14001 Environmental Management Systems printer

 A catalogue record for this book is available from the National Library of Australia

ISBN 978 1 76134 622 4

penguin.com.au

We at Penguin Random House Australia acknowledge that Aboriginal and Torres Strait Islander peoples are the Traditional Custodians and the first storytellers of the lands on which we live and work. We honour Aboriginal and Torres Strait Islander peoples' continuous connection to Country, waters, skies and communities. We celebrate Aboriginal and Torres Strait Islander stories, traditions and living cultures; and we pay our respects to Elders past and present.

To my children, who made me the mother I am, and to my late father, who would be proud of me for having the words to inspire those in the throes of parenthood.

Contents

Preface		1
Chapter 1	Ground zero: The birth	27
Chapter 2	The hours after the birth	51
Chapter 3	The first twenty-four hours	71
Chapter 4	Feeding	97
Chapter 5	The (very) early days	121
Chapter 6	Home time – the first week	141
Chapter 7	The days are long but the years are short – the first month	175
Chapter 8	Survival mode – the first three months	209
Chapter 9	Sleep and settling	245
Chapter 10	What we can learn from other countries	267

Notes	279
Acknowledgements	283
Index	289

Preface

The fourth trimester is rough, but beautiful. Challenging, but rewarding. Exhausting, but fulfilling. Indefinite, but short. You will not just be physically and emotionally challenged for the next twelve or so weeks, you'll be mentally challenged too. Gee, I started that off in a positive manner, didn't I? Generally, by the time you hit home, the happy hormones and adrenaline have worn off . . . you are still madly in love with what you have just created, but things are starting to taper down. Reality sets in and you begin to realise that what lies ahead for the next few months is constant nappy changes, never-ending walks to dispose of them in the outside bin and countless hours feeding your baby, whether that be via the breast or the bottle. The thing is, no one really delves into the fourth trimester.

Not birthing classes, not your mum, not your midwife or obstetrician; it really is unknown territory. I bet you barely even knew it was a thing.

I am here to break it down for you. Before I begin, I'd like to warn you ... some will swim through it unscathed and wonder what the hell all the commotion was about; others (most of us) will turn to water and at some point need a lifeguard to pull them up for air.

It's long nights and slow days. Unfinished meals and midnight snacks. It's cold coffee and toast scraps. Sore boobs and sore bums. Love handles and flabby bits. Headaches and water refills. Missed calls and unanswered texts. Netflix subscriptions and popcorn for dinner. Empty washing powder and piles of laundry. Imposing visitors and empty food cupboards. Needy animals and full arms. Tender hearts and yearning for more. Forgetting yourself and feeling invisible. Prioritising everything but minimising your needs. Healing your body yet stretching yourself more than ever before.

I guess this begs the question why I have decided to write a book on the fourth trimester and share some of my tried-and-true wisdom with you, all the while being absolutely stretched myself. Well, the truth is, I can't help it. Write, that is. Sharing my words and personal knowledge with you all is cathartic for me.

The fourth trimester is rough, but beautiful. Challenging, but rewarding. Exhausting, but fulfilling. Indefinite, but short. You will not just be physically and emotionally challenged . . . you'll be mentally challenged too.

The Fourth Trimester

I have more than 20,000 people tune in every day to hear my stories, witness my shitshow of a messy house, observe me juggling and dropping all the balls in real time and thanking me for being so damn 'real' and 'normal' and 'not fake', when social media can be full of unrealistic, staged, bogus, 'perfect' lives, kids, mothers and households.

I say it how it is. I always have and I always will. I am perfectly *very* imperfect and I guess that's what makes me stand out like a sore thumb in the highlight reels of social media. But there is more to me than that.

First and foremost, I am a mumma of four bebes . . . Alfie, nine, my sensitive dreamboat mumma's boy; Essie, seven, my mature, fiery, independent sass queen; Coco, four, my spirit animal, she will rule the world one day; and Scout, twelve months, my fourth lucky charm. My relaxed, happy, pull-me-in-every-direction-without-bother child. Will there be more? The million-dollar question. I can't imagine never being pregnant again nor birthing a baby again, especially given how much I cherish the slow and long days the fourth trimester can bring . . . time will tell. I am not done Today, but perhaps Tomorrow I might be. My blessings are written in the sky.

When I am not baby making, I am a registered midwife and have been for the past ten years. Pregnancy and childbirth will always have my heart,

Preface

making the birth suite my favourite place to be in my working week. If you can even call it that. I am also a qualified sleep consultant. I can proudly say that my sleep business has grown exponentially for all the right reasons. The importance of sleep for everyone is *so* underrated, and for babies postpartum, sleep is a necessity for survival. Our growing team currently sends our sleepy magic all over the globe and we have thousands of well-rested babies, mummas and families because of it.

After the birth of my third baby, Coco, I found I was absolutely loving breastfeeding the third time around. But I couldn't help feeling a twinge of guilt that breastfeeding was so easy for me, when my Instagram was flooded with desperate mothers seeking breastfeeding support. It drove me to want to learn about breastfeeding in greater depth than my midwife training had provided, so I studied lactation consulting for a year, sat a four-hour exam and became a certified IBCLC (International Board of Certified Lactation Consultants). Despite having all of these studies and credentials behind me, one thing is certain: I am not a doctor. I have never studied medicine (if I had my time again I would train to be an obstetrician) and therefore nothing I write in this wonderful book is to be taken as medical advice. Take it more as a sister sharing advice with a sister, or a grandma or mumma telling their daughter wonderful words of insight. Basically, I'm sharing some everyday 'common sense' – that doesn't seem to be so common these days – from one midwife mumma to another fresh, fragile mumma and family. Four kids down, with a successful business, a happy home and busy life, I do hope you take away some lovely sentiments from this book and, even more, find yourself more capable of catching your breath in the moments during the fourth trimester when you might feel like you are drowning.

My birth experience

Giving birth is hard; and as I was settling into the fourth trimester for a fourth time, in a hospital ward about to face three *very* excited kids awaiting my arrival from the birth suite with a baby in my arms, I have to admit that I asked myself, *Holy hell. Where is the pause and rewind button?* I should have listened to my midwife and stayed longer recovering post-birth. The fourth trimester certainly hits different each time you enter it.

This time around mine followed a long, drawn-out labour. The birth of my third babe, Coco, had been a dream. In for an induction at 1.30 pm ... baby born around 6 pm after officially going into labour two and

Preface

a half hours prior. A precipitate birth they call that. Under four hours from the onset of labour to birthing babe. Quick, hard and perfect with my epidural. Scout, on the other hand, I thought would fly out. The more babes you have doesn't necessarily mean a quicker labour and birth.

So there I was this time around, legs wide open, bleeding post-birth waiting for my placenta to deliver, when the fourth trimester officially smacked me in the face with a baby that wasn't breathing (thanks anxiety meds) and an adrenaline-filled body that could not stop shaking. Birth is wild. My first five minutes into the 'golden' trimester was filled with panic and a desperation to hold and feed her. She needed her mumma and I needed her more.

That five minutes felt like an eternity . . . finally . . . relief. She cried. I was at last able to take a look at my baby's face, her tiny ten fingers and littler ten toes. She was everything and more. Nine months of growing her. Nurturing her. Waiting for her. She was finally here. My heart doubled in size, just like my swollen flaps. It was love at first sight.

She was a girl. She was alert and she was *hungry*.

I wasn't in any mood to do the 'breast crawl' . . . I was dead tired and she was flapping around like a duck with plucked wings so I guided her to the boob and she latched like a leech, not letting go for an eternity. In fact, all this time later and she hasn't left her fave spot.

My placenta finally detached from my throbbing uterus like a champ and slid out in one piece. It was officially over. My fourth pregnancy and birth done and dusted. Just like that. If it was over in the blink of an eye, isn't it so fascinating we are meant to adapt to this new world together like nothing terribly important happened?

Birth can be beautiful as well as an ordeal. It's exhilarating yet arduous. It's slow but over so quickly. It's your body being filled with a big bunch of hormones (natural and sometimes synthetic) and asking it to perform a certain task in a certain amount of time. It's being cut open, through layers upon layers of muscle and tissue, to dissect your baby's home and bring them out into the world through your stomach. Caesarean mummas, you are beyond brilliant. Strong, resilient and tenacious. Yet here we are, in this day and age, expected to heal from such an ordeal like it's a stubbed toe and sent home a day or two post-birth. Isn't that beyond insane?

I am grateful my body was able to birth vaginally four times. I am such a pussy I wouldn't be able to handle the pain after a caesarean section. I would send myself and everyone around me senile with my whingeing if I was unable to sprint off the couch to get my tenth chocolate bar for the morning.

Preface

I have my beautiful ob to thank for my lovely births and intact perineum. What a guy. I could never imagine loving any man other than my partner, yet here I am, mourning the fact I may never see him again, if Scout is my last ever baby.

There isn't enough acknowledgement of the bond between birthing mother and caregiver. Whether it is a unicorn midwife who is everything plus more to you, or a godsend of an obstetrician . . . regardless of the gender, they become your confidant, your safe place, you and your baby's lifeline throughout the nine months of pregnancy. And once you birth your baby, that relationship is essentially over. Believe it or not, you will mourn this relationship as you now have to navigate raising your baby in the outside world without their guidance. It's a different time in your life, no doubt about it.

So, there I was, lying in my own birth juices with a side of turd, a baby suckling away like the leech she was. Probably more like a piranha if I am being honest. I have no idea how something with a mouth no bigger than a ten cent piece can suck the life out of your nipples, leaving them for dead. But Scout can, that's for sure. It was a sign that for the next six weeks – not to mention the next sixteen years of her life – we were in this together. Without me, she had nothing. Legit.

How is that for pressure? At the same time, her dad,

my wonderful partner Ambrose, sat back comfortably in a chair sending the fam happy snaps of his third girl and fourth child, secretly a little disappointed she hadn't come out with a doodle like he'd anticipated.

I vividly remember him laughing without a care in the world as he sculled his coffee in between answering phone calls with excited family members. I, on the other hand, was wondering if my ob had shoved enough Panadol and Voltaren up my ass to allow me to survive my first shower without feeling like my insides were falling out.

In this moment, I knew things were already changing. It had already started. The resentment that Ambrose was free, independent, able to move around in the world without anything stuck to his nipple and harbouring no primal urge to cling to that baby for dear life in fear that something might happen to her.

The maternal instincts hit differently. They just do and don't try to tell me otherwise. It is like we mums are programmed to cling to our cubs the second they are born and struggle to let our guard down at any time. Sure, Ambrose and most partners will do anything to protect their children, but it's the mothers that make their family a tribe. The mother–child bond is a code no one can break.

The time had finally come to part with my baby after nine long months. The first time ever I placed

Preface

the responsibility of caring for our child in someone else's hands. The first time our skin-to-skin would be broken. It sounds unhinged, doesn't it? But it's true. I carried her for nine months, so safe and secure, and now Ambrose would hold her for the first time without me. I always feel strange handing my baby over for the first time, but she would be just as safe in her dadda's big warm arms as she was in mine. After all, she is the other half of him too. As I wrapped her up tight before handing her to Ambrose, a little noise escaped her mouth; she sounded like a kitten. I started to tear up. I knew this was what love felt like again. While I was busy staring into her eyes, with Ambrose rushing me for a cuddle of her, a juicy clot landed on my pad to remind me it was time to get up and shower.

Right, I told myself, *I can do this. Get up jelly legs.* My other kids were already at the hospital desperately waiting to meet this new little person and my pad was *wayyyyy* overdue for a change. I hobbled to the toilet, the afterbirth blood trickling down my inner thigh; just another reminder it was all over. I turned the shower on super hot; I couldn't wait to drown my achy back and vjj in the heat. As I sat back in the hospital chair thoughtfully placed beneath the shower head, closed my eyes and dowsed myself in the flowing water, I naturally went to cradle my belly, only to realise it was no longer there. This part always hurt me the most. I guess because my heart always asks, *Is this the last time?*

My once firm, round belly was now jiggly and soft, staring at me all flabby and empty. Vacant. My uterus already hiding away. I no longer had a shower companion with me as I had earlier that morning. I was alone. It was just me again. It was my new reality and soon to be my new normal once more.

As I closed my eyes and washed myself, I became temporarily lost reminiscing about the birth, almost like it was a dream I was yet to wake up from. It was a lovely feeling, a fleeting moment, an oversaturation of all the wonderful hormones flooding my body and an awakening to what lay ahead. Instead of showering with a baby in my belly, from now on I would be showering with my ears on high alert and phantom cries drawing me out of the shower before I even had time to wash myself. The anxiety of what lay ahead dawned on me. *Just keep swimming. Just keep swimming. Just keep swimming.*

My peaceful post-birth shower was rudely interrupted by a squawking baby and a partner tapping on the door to ask 'How much longer?' until I was finished. Reality check right there.

In true mum form, still dripping after I failed to dry myself properly in my rush, I struggled to pull my pants on. My baby needed me and I felt every inch of that.

Preface

I whacked a granny nappy on, slipped my saggy colostrum-filled titties into my too tight maternity crop and burst out that door as if someone was holding a gun to my head. 'Mumma is here,' I whispered to bub as I scooped her out of Ambrose's arms. I sat in a chair and began feeding her, at the same time fending off a thousand texts pinging on my phone. 'The kids are waiting,' Ambrose reminded me. I shut my eyes for a moment, took a deep breath and imagined their reaction to meeting their sister. I felt excited . . . but also nervous. 'Just let me finish feeding, I will be a moment' . . . and right then and there I knew, there were no truer words spoken. These words would frequent my mouth from here on in for a long time to come.

I finished her feed, swaddled her tightly, placed her in the bassinet and took one last look around the room that had witnessed my fourth birth. I slowly pushed her bassinet out of the birth suite, taking the big step into the next part of the fourth trimester – the postnatal ward. As I approached my room, Ambrose following with loads of luggage, I could hear my three other kids giggling as they waited so patiently for the door to open. I had dreamed of this moment.

As the doors opened so did my heart. My four children all together for the first time. Their smiles, their laughter, their happiness. All worth it after sixteen weeks of morning sickness and ten weeks of an

---

Birth can be beautiful as well as an ordeal. It's exhilarating yet arduous. It's slow but over so quickly.

Preface

irritable uterus. It had been a challenging pregnancy at times, yet here I was already questioning when I could have another.

Oxytocin, the love hormone, is insane. It can swallow you in its massive love bubble and have you temporarily fooled that nothing in this world is a bother or too hard to handle. I wish we could bottle that hormone up and keep it safe for when we need it most.

The kids spent two hours fighting over whose turn it was to hold the baby and who could sit on my lap in between. It was getting late, the kids were becoming stroppy, I was exhausted. They kissed bub goodbye and gave me a tight squeeze as I assured them they could come back in the morning as soon as they woke. The door shut behind them and I breathed a sigh of relief. How much more could I take today? I was ready for bed, bub was ready for her next feed and it was late. I had barely slept the night before as I'd been too excited and nervous, but I could feel my adrenaline starting to dwindle as it was about to tick over to a new day. After the feed I switched the lights off, closed my eyes and bam – in typical hospital patient fashion – the door opened with a midwife wanting to do my observations before I went to sleep for the night. Really? At midnight? I had to remind myself that I too was a midwife, often doing the exact same thing.

The Fourth Trimester

I woke the next morning to a little baby hiccupping as she stared at me through her bassinet. The sun was peeking through the blind and I could hear the breakfast trolley making its way up the corridor. I was *starving*. Who am I kidding. I am always hungry. I knew I had to lap up this one-on-one time with bub with no other children around so I kept reminding myself to be patient, take it slow, the next few days at least wouldn't come with a rule book.

I think that is an important reminder for everyone who is about to venture into the fourth trimester – there certainly isn't a rule book, nor anyone sitting beside you to instruct your every move on how to parent.

Scout did nothing but feed, feed, feed. It was all day, every day for a solid week. Not only did she bring my milk in reasonably quickly, she turned it into a tsunami. My flow would drown her each feed, followed by several burps, a little spew and a fuss to be swaddled and go back to sleep. This was essentially my first three weeks of mothering Scout.

I left hospital on day four, a day early . . . I know what you are thinking. How silly of me. Ambrose wrangled the older three into hospital where they ran up the hallway screaming with joy, no doubt waking every other patient and their baby along the way to collect Scout and me. I immediately felt overwhelmed.

Preface

I was beyond tired from the broken sleep, but I pushed through as the kids were so excited. All I wanted was to get home, sit at the bottom of the shower and give my hair and body a good wash. I wanted fresh clothes, clean sheets and a cuppa in front of the TV. You will soon work out it's the little things that matter the most.

The arrival home was a brutal reminder that I was once again walking into at least a year of broken sleep and night feeds, unsettled toddler bedtimes and late nights with my older two. Generally around this period of exhaustion my baby blues set in. I waited and waited and waited, but this time, they never arrived. I am not sure if that's a good or bad thing, but I'll take it as a win.

The first two nights home were particularly awful. When the baby fed, Coco woke and sat next to her trying to link arms with me and have chats about Barbie and Ken. It felt like I was stuck in hell. Between trying to keep my eyes awake and maintain a good latch with the baby, and Coco kicking and screaming like a maniac when I told her she wasn't allowed to play with her Barbie house at 4 am, I knew this transition to home life was going to be a little tougher than the others. Essentially I had two little babies again, both desperately needing their mumma.

No one actually divulges the real truth about adapting to your new family life at home. No one. The highs, the lows, the in-betweens. I knew it was going to be a long few weeks, but it helped to keep reminding myself, just like I do with all new mummas, that slow and steady wins the race. Expectations reset back to zero and the aim of the game is to make it through to bedtime.

The visitors we had from the moment we got home from hospital were appreciated but intense. We both come from big families so I knew there would be a lot of people dropping by, but I honestly thought by the fourth baby everyone's baby fever would have disappeared... how wrong was I! It was peak summer so not only did we have people coming and going to meet the baby, we also had a pool constantly full of swimmers. It was a lot of fun but in hindsight, way too much for a mum and baby entering the fourth trimester. So much for rest. I should have utilised my full stay in hospital. Every day counts. Keep that in mind if you are going to birth your second, third, fourth, fifth, tenth baby. Don't rush home.

Aside from constant breastfeeds, the first week at home saw us with endless wet and dirty nappies. Poo explosions were on the reg, Napisan was running on empty and the washing machine was getting a massive workout. How could one teeny tiny person add so much laundry to the basket? Crazy! My housework was piling up but I couldn't muster the energy to

Preface

do too much. Thank god for the grandparents. They secretly loved coming over and 'folding' the washing. Any excuse to be close to the new baby. I would never decline their help. There was something wonderful about their ability to turn my overwhelm to calm by just walking through the door. It's not lost on me how lucky my family is to have so much help when so many don't really have anyone at all.

The first week, in typical newborn fashion, saw Scout sleeping her days away and partying all night. Probably a newborn parent's main complaint in the early stages of parenthood. *Ha*. I knew it would pass. But I had to remind myself of this as it's something I discuss with my patients and sleep clients regularly. I will go into depth about newborn sleep and settling in Chapter 9.

At the same time, Scout's skin resembled a teenager's; with her newborn pimples we couldn't get a nice photo of the poor thing. Week one we also had our health nurse visit us at home for Scout's weigh-in. The poor woman would have thought my house was a spectacle. We had kids running around ... some cousins, some from the street and some next-door neighbours. We had Grandma in the kitchen doing the dishes. Ambrose was outside in the pool with some mates having a beer, and me, make-up free and gaunt sitting on the couch talking about my postpartum bleeding and the bedlam that is having four kids. She too was a mum of four kids so completely understood where I was at. I had a great relationship with all my health nurses. They have always been so beautiful and non-judgemental, so it makes me sad when people describe feeling misunderstood and condemned by theirs. It is the opposite of what should happen.

Week two greeted us with a nice random five-hour block of sleep, which I knew would be a one-off, but couldn't help hoping it wasn't. One can only wish. Scout had now sorted out her days and nights, which was brill and allowed me to feel more in control than the week before. Ambrose and I had barely come up for air, speaking what seemed like just a few words to each other over the last week. Not out of spite, just out of pure craziness. Like ships in the night we passed each other in the hallway.

Coco had settled down at night and was back to sleeping through, and all of a sudden I just had one baby, not two, which was a big relief. I ventured out on my own to the shops for a massage. It was bloody bliss. Warranted. Well-deserved if I say so myself. One thing I promised myself this pregnancy was that when baby was born I was going to let go of some control in order to keep my cup semi-full. I know how important this is. It was only an hour and a half but damn it felt good and made me a better mother when I returned home.

Preface

We had our second health nurse visit followed by Scout's first proper outing to the beach. She celebrated with a car screaming session that saw me pull over several times to pacify her. It was awesome. Between her tears, bubba was still as sleepy as ever, only ever opening her eyes for a brief moment, then closing them again to return to her sweet slumber. The kids kept asking why she was so boring. 'When will she wake up Mum?' I knew in the next week or two she would wake up to the world and then the period of baby sleep would change significantly. For now, I was going to enjoy this time of rest.

Week three was a game changer. Scout was in the basic routine of breastfeed, play (nappy change/mat/tummy time) and sleep. Repeated every three or so hours. We also had our first growth spurt, which saw two days of being glued to the tit, but it wasn't all bad ... it meant she had a few big blocks of sleep the following nights. Our Scouty bum did indeed wake up to the world and began practising lots more smiling and focusing her eyes. Babies' increased alertness at this age is due to the melatonin leaving their system that was once created by their placenta. It is responsible for their sleepy and wakeful periods. There was no doubt about it, it was time for Scout to start producing her own hormones, which start with awake time in the daylight and sleepy time in a dark room.

The Fourth Trimester

Cue me calling every blind supplier to ask if they could urgently install blackout blinds for her room. If you know you know and if you don't, stay tuned . . . I will chat more about this in Chapter 9.

My postpartum bleeding was still making itself known. I wished it would make its mind up. One minute I had thrown all my pads out and the next minute I was scrambling my bag and car for a spare one as the red river decided to drench my undies at the most inconvenient time. It is such a thrill being a female isn't it.

My boobs were starting to settle, which was brilliant . . . Scout and my clothing had definitely had enough of the torrential leaking. Around this time, lo and behold, our not-so-lovely friend colic made an appearance. Colic, despite not being an illness or a disease, is a bastard to deal with. It's a thing your baby does, like cry, belch, vom, fart, arch and squirm while the milk tries to settle in their tummy. Fourth time around, 'is it colic or reflux' was still my number one search in my Google browser. How hilarious. It certainly doesn't get any easier each time. Or maybe it does, just not for me.

Chemist Warehouse took all my money. I bought every colic remedy on the shelf. How silly of me. I was well aware that fixing my feeding first would drastically help the colic. Anyway, it is safe to say Infacol has my heart now.

Fourth time around, 'is it colic or reflux' was still my number one search in my Google browser.

The Fourth Trimester

As week four came to light, the nights and days rolled into one. The circus started to calm ever so slightly and the elation of having a new sibling had started to die down (thank god). The happy hormones had certainly turned into the just-keep-swimming hormones and there was no doubt about it, this mumma was *tireddddddddddddd*.

School was back in full swing, which meant routine and lunch boxes and childcare were officially back. Hallelujah! This meant I could get a minute to myself and even sneak in a mid-morning nap. My god how I needed one of them. It also provided me with a chance to actually hold and look at my baby. I don't think I had had a look in with her, apart from with a breast in her mouth, since she was born.

We had our third weigh-in with the health nurse and, my goodness, little piggy is porky for a reason. No wonder she is riddled with colic, the poor love. I began to *really* make a conscious effort to focus on my breastfeeding. No more being lazy. Time to resort to feeding laying on my back so the milk would stop drowning her. And guess what? It bloody worked!! Her colic died down super quick and she was a much more settled, content baby. *Ahhhh*, I felt like I could breathe for a moment. Anyone with a colicky/reflux baby will understand the anxiety a distressed baby causes. Not only do you feel terribly sorry for them,

Preface

you also feel so guilty that you could be the cause of it. Motherhood really is a roller-coaster.

Week five came around and our baby was slowly coming out of the real newborn stage. Her cry was a little different. She wasn't as fragile. She was getting stronger. Her patience was slowly extending. Life began feeling a tad easier.

Routine was evolving . . . I bathed Scout at the same time every night, fed at the same time most evenings and Scout had the same blocks of sleep most nights. It was groundhog day and I was okay with that. I knew from experience that it was only temporary and that by the end of three months we would well and truly have found our groove.

CHAPTER 1

Ground zero: The birth

Welcome to the new ... everything

New life. Not just for your baby, but for you also. I bet you never thought that the moment your baby was placed on your chest was the moment a new you was going to be born. Welcome to your new life. To the new you. To the new us. The new everything. The fourth trimester, something that you were probably unaware even existed. You know that moment you meet your baby for the first time, that very second? That is where it all begins. As if giving birth wasn't enough, you are then forced to navigate this happy medium with a blindfold on after being spun 110 times in a circle.

Throw in lumpy tits, blood trickling down your inner thighs and a bruised ego and there you have it, motherhood in all its glory. Now it's time to enter the fourth trimester.

The birth

But let's start with the birth. The place where the fourth trimester greets you as your baby is pushed or pulled out of your vjj or plucked straight out of your once tight tummy that now resembles a beautifully cooked pork belly from a three-hat restaurant. This is the reality of birth. It ain't always pretty despite being 'beautiful' . . . in fact, a lot of the time it's not, and that's okay apart from the times when it is not. Park that birth trauma at the back of your mind, we can address this later in depth. For now, it's pork belly and tender bruised perineums on the fourth trimester menu.

It is actually a little surprising if you think of birth as a natural event to consider that according to the Australian Institute of Health and Welfare the number of women having vaginal births has decreased and caesarean sections increased over the last decade or so.

Of course, there are *so* many factors that come into play here: birthrates, age, fertility, multiple births, personal choice, baby presentation (breech birth, for

Ground zero: the birth

example, when the feet or bottom come out first), pregnancy complications, induction of labour that can turn into an emergency caesarean section. The list goes on. I feel like a completely *normal* (what even is that these days?) vaginal birth is pretty rare. Despite the number of assisted vaginal births remaining fairly stable (as the AIHW rates show), it is still no fun having a forceps or vacuum-assisted delivery or even a little episiotomy *but* I am a firm believer that all of these modes of delivery absolutely have a time and place and can be lifesaving options. There is just so much to labour and birth that often isn't mentioned in birth classes.

I like to think of myself as a modern midwife, keeping up with the times. Despite wishing every single person had a straightforward vaginal birth, we know this just isn't going to be the case. As midwives and patients, we can keep advocating for this, but for many valid reasons it's not always possible. Not everything will run smoothly – get used to that in the fourth trimester – but if you can do anything for yourself as a pregnant or new mumma, research and educate yourself so that you can advocate for yourself and your baby when the time comes. But let's get to the good stuff. The moments you have been waiting nine months for.

The initial few hours post-birth will see you with

The Fourth Trimester

a baby trying to latch to your boob (hopefully easily for your sake), blood dripping from your vjj in ebbs and flows (even if you have had a caesarean) and a midwife fussing over you to make sure you remain nice and healthy post-birth. A blood pressure cuff will be your latest annoyance, not to mention being subjected to regular fundal rubs (in other words, the good old uterus rub) that midwives have to perform ever so frequently post-birth to make sure your uterus is playing the right game and going back into the hiding spot where it used to live before you fell pregnant. If you were one of the lucky ones to have an IV drip inserted (providing you and bub with adequate additional hydration and extra medicine if need be), you will be counting down the minutes until you can yank that thing out, and if you had the added bonus of a catheter (a *teeeeny* long fine tube inserted into your urethra to drain your wee for you – yep you heard it here first), *woweeeeee* that little tug aggravating you down there will probably be starting to feel really annoying and you will be begging for a tube-free shower in peace, shaky legs and all.

If you are birthing in the public system, your labour bed will be calling for a new patient the moment your baby's head pops out, so time is certainly of the essence for you all. You may be lucky enough to smother your baby skin-to-skin for a solid hour or

Ground zero: the birth

more post-delivery, and that is ideal if you can. Your midwife will be trying their best to accommodate this as they too know how precious this time is. In a perfect world we would have unlimited labour beds and midwives and nurses who could cuddle you up in an oxytocin bubble and drown you with all the love and TLC you so rightly deserve after bringing your baby into being. The reality is, we live in such an incredibly busy baby-making world that women in the public system are lucky to get twenty-four hours in hospital for a normal vaginal birth before being forced home to mother their new child, hopefully equipped with a little confidence that they know something about what lies ahead, but in fact many soon learn that actually they know absolutely nothing, or at least a lot less than first anticipated.

Caesarean birth

I know you are dying to know the lowdown between a scheduled caesarean section versus an emergency one, their implications and how you will recover from both.

First off, a scheduled section is just that: your baby's birth scheduled at a certain time and date, born via an operation. These births are super chill (most of the time, if the parents aren't too nervous) and tend to

As if giving birth wasn't enough ... throw in lumpy tits, blood trickling down your inner thighs and a bruised ego and there you have it, motherhood in all its glory.

Ground zero: the birth

go seamlessly with a standard recovery. As a midwife, I see these as straightforward births that usually transition easily into the postpartum period.

An emergency section is a different story. Despite medically being labelled this, it does not necessarily mean it is an absolute 'emergency'. I will give you two examples. A real emergency section could be if a mother was in labour and all of a sudden the baby becomes distressed (known as fetal distress) and struggles to recover, therefore needing urgent delivery. In this situation, an emergency caesarean section is required. Example two, which isn't an emergency as such but is still deemed an emergency section, is when the patient has been booked in for a caesarean section but her waters break prior to her scheduled operation. Despite the baby being well and not needing urgent delivery, this will be classified as an emergency caesarean section because she will need to be taken to theatre to deliver by caesarean section, *unless* mumma ends up trialling a normal birth or VBAC (vaginal birth after caesarean section) as approved by her doctor.

If you are having a scheduled caesarean section in the public system or end up having an emergency section, your time in hospital will be an average of three nights (if you are lucky), all dependent on whether the beds are full or not. After your baby has been born, they will be placed onto your chest for a delicious meet and greet then whisked away to have their immunisations, cord clamped and baby check before being reunited with you to hopefully achieve more skin-to-skin contact and lots of mumma and daddy cuddles. You will feel like you are in a movie, a dream perhaps . . . it's all lights, camera, action in the operating theatre, but you won't care, you will be floating on a cloud of strong meds intertwined with your own delightful oxytocin birth hormones and gawking at this baby that was living in your stomach ten minutes ago and is now cuddled up on your chest, right where they are meant to be. Time feels like it is standing still, a lifetime of being flat on your back unable to move your legs, but in fact it is all over within an hour, when you will be transferred to a recovery bay to continue your care and feed your baby for the first time if you were unable to in theatre, which unfortunately is super likely.

Once you are well enough, you will be transferred to your postnatal bed where you will spend the next few days healing from your operation and bonding with your baby. You will be chowing down pain meds to dull the caesarean wound ache and encouraged to gently walk around the ward to gain strength and increase blood flow to your legs and throughout your body. Somehow you'll need to muster the strength to do this all on your own when you head home – recover, feed, medicate, regulate, breathe, cry (hopefully happy tears) and look after yourself and your baby with the help of your partner and family unit. It's all a lot. But you can do it and you will do it. Not because you necessarily want to, but because we are wired to.

See how not straightforward birth can be despite sounding so easy and straightforward? All of these factors contribute to a mother's recovery and how she enters the fourth trimester. And in my experience as a midwife, I've seen that in many more cases than not, new mums are completely underprepared for the essential recovery that lies ahead.

Home birth

In Australia, home birthrates are on the increase, which is wonderful for those who yearn to birth safely in their own surroundings. The beauty of birthing at home is that your birth naturally blends into the fourth trimester that follows. You aren't going from one place to the next, you are in your natural fourth trimester from start to finish, the place you feel safest and most comfortable, sharing the love with your new baby and family. Life is good. If you have opted to birth at home with your midwives and nearest and dearest, how beautiful is that? I hope your birth is or was as dreamy as you imagined and that you embrace the subtle move to the fourth trimester with open arms from your loved ones.

If it all sounds so wonderful, why on earth isn't everyone birthing at home? There is no simple answer. Mostly it's to do with the safety of mother and baby during labour and birth, the lack of support medically, a lack of funding from government and a lack of skilled, competent home-birth midwives. In 2022, only a small portion of women in Australia (0.5 per cent) birthed at home safely with the assistance of a registered midwife. This is vastly different to many other countries. In the UK the Office for National Statistics reported that in 2020, 2.4 per cent of women in England and Wales gave birth at home.

To increase the rate of successful, safe, home-birth rates in Australia, a lot needs to be done. More hospital home-birth programs need to be available, there needs to be a higher threshold for acceptable clientele, more highly skilled midwives employed, more incentives to birth at home if deemed safe and appropriate, and a *lot* of education for both hospital staff (should an emergency arise) and of course the mother herself.

Emergency situations are also a very real thing and need to be closely considered when opting for a home birth. What if an emergency arises mid-labour and mum and baby need urgent attention? Can this be provided at home or do mum and baby need to

Ground zero: the birth

be transferred to their nearest hospital as soon as possible? So many questions and so many variables. As a midwife and a mum, I just hope those birthing at home have excellent, trained support and achieve the best possible outcome for themselves and their unborn babies.

Birth trauma

Firstly, I want to emphasise that I am not qualified to counsel women and their families about birth trauma. That being said, I am very passionate about preventing it and helping those affected receive the correct treatment post-birth to recover as much as they can from it. One of the fundamental reasons I have written this book is that I strongly believe education on the realities of labour and birth and what potentially lies ahead for your postnatal experience should begin as early as possible, even prior to conception.

The information relating to birth trauma in this section might be difficult reading for some women, particularly the examples I've provided below, so please look after yourself and skip over anything that you feel might be triggering for you. I truly hope that this section contains some helpful advice though, and if you are reading this and you think you have birth trauma, I urge you to seek appropriate assistance. You do not have to suffer in silence. A debrief about your birth and concerns is essential and has the added benefit of enabling care providers to be educated along the way.

If you are reading this pregnant, yet to birth, please don't think every single person suffers from birth trauma. Statistics in Australia report one in three women have identified their birthing experience as traumatic; however, this does not mean it will necessarily be you. For those of you reading who have already birthed and fit into this category, firstly, I am sorry. I am sorry you feel traumatised by your birthing experience, and I am sorry you can't redo it. Birth trauma is a real thing. It is distressingly prevalent in our society, which should not be the case. Birth trauma is complicated as it is subjective and personal to each and every birthing mother or partner. Unfortunately, the number of women reporting birth trauma is increasing, which is alarming, but not all that surprising.

It is important to also note that there is a vast difference between a 'difficult' or 'complicated' birth and actual birth trauma, which is described as physical, emotional or psychological trauma for not only the mother or partner but also the baby.

Did the mother or baby experience actual physical trauma from the birth? For example, baby has a

One in three women have identified their birthing experience as traumatic.

broken collarbone from a complicated shoulder dystocia delivery or mum experienced an episiotomy extending to her anus causing her immense physical and emotional pain. Or is the trauma on an emotional or psychological level, resulting in emotional distress or PTSD (post-traumatic stress disorder). Does the trauma extend beyond the physical labour and birthing process? The list goes on. Perhaps you have been unlucky enough to experience such birth trauma yourself and know of the negative impact it can have on your fourth trimester and postpartum experience.

Most trauma, of course, cannot be prevented. In my work as a midwife I've cared for a mother who has just been told her baby's heart is no longer beating while still inside her. That trauma, heartbreak and loss is palpable. These experiences traumatise the patient as well as her partner, who can sometimes be forgotten or left behind in these difficult situations.

Today, more than ever before, women are speaking up about their birth trauma and strongly advocating for more awareness, education, support and funding to access external services from GPs, psychologists, psychiatrists and counsellors. There *is* help available. Should you experience trauma in childbirth, I shower you with so much virtual love. I wish nothing more than for you to be healed and freed of your trauma. It starts with a visit to your GP and a debrief with your

Ground zero: the birth

hospital. From there I hope you have been directed to appropriate care providers and resources that will help you on the path towards healing.

Your birthing team

The midwife
Did you know that the word 'midwife' means 'with woman'? Well, what can I say? We are the best of the best, no doubt about it; we're there to ensure you have the safest birth possible. We champion you during your labour and birth or caesarean section. We look after your physical health during labour and after you have had your baby, and sometimes, if you are in the public system, we even visit you at home post-birth. In the hospital we are your confidant, your caregiver, your cheerleader, your number one fan. All we care about is that you and your baby are well and thriving as best you can. Postnatally we can help shower you, dress you, assist you to breastfeed, check your wounds and bumps and lumps, keep you pain-free and comfortable, monitor your mental health, keep you both alive and hopefully have wonderful words of wisdom to give you the confidence to dominate motherhood like the legend you are as you commence your fourth trimester.

The Fourth Trimester

You will have several midwives attending to you from the moment you enter hospital. One or two for your labour and birth or caesarean, then many on the postnatal ward. The in-charge will try to assign you the same midwife as much as possible so you can get some continuity of care during your postnatal period, which has unsurprisingly proven to be the most satisfying option for patient care. During your postnatal stay your midwife will take your observations regularly (monitoring heart rate, respiratory rate, blood pressure, temperature) and also check your fundus (uterus) to make sure it is going back to its normal pre-pregnancy position. They will also monitor your blood loss, check for swelling in your legs, closely look at your caesarean section wound or perineum to ensure they are healing correctly and assist you with your breastfeeding. They will help you with your baby's first bath and do their best to educate you on all things postpartum. Basically, anytime you have a question, query, concern or need assistance, you buzz for your midwife. Midwives not only have your physical health on their mind, they are concerned with your emotional and mental health also. They are your reassuring referral service and a shoulder to cry on. Essentially, a giant hug in human form.

Not only does your midwife care for you, the mumma, they also care for their other little patient,

Ground zero: the birth

your baby. They are always checking your baby is healthy, feeding well and has adequate output (urine and poo). They also perform observations on bub to monitor heart rate, respiratory rate, temperature and oxygen saturation and to confirm overall that they are thriving. They give the newborn any necessary needles, check weight, look out for any abnormalities, and make referrals if they have any concerns. Midwives really are like supercalifragilistic brilliant mini doctors, but better, more attentive and nurturing ... *ha* ... just without the med school and hefty pay.

And our love doesn't stop there. We think about you when we get home and hope you and baby are growing beautifully together. To this day I remember most of my patients and often wonder what they are doing all these years later. If we are blessed and the timing is right, I often get to continue my care of them through subsequent pregnancies and births.

I don't think anyone who has a baby forgets their midwife. And that is a good thing I hope. For my first birth, Alfie's, I had a total of six midwives throughout the day during my labour and birth. One who admitted me to the birth suite for my induction. Another who cared for me during the morning shift. One who jumped in to support me during my midwife's lunch-break. One for the afternoon shift and a further two who assisted beside my obstetrician during Alfie's long, hard descent into this world. For Essie's birth I had a gorgeous midwife who admitted me at 2 am, then two other midwives for the birth assisting my ob. For Coco, I had one lovely midwife for the whole duration of my labour and birth. She was brilliant! And another assisted with her birth also. Then with Scout bum, who took forever to birth for a fourth baby, I had three midwives and two students. How lucky are we as mummas to have this level of care during our births and hospital stays? I wish Australia could be more like the Netherlands where new mums have a midwife visiting every day for a week post-birth at home for lots of TLC, support and education. Nonetheless, as a mum, I am forever grateful for our beautiful, hardworking middies.

The obstetrician
The pregnancy specialist! The guru of complications. The hero of your safe birth. They are fabulous and we are lucky to have them. Let's be real, they may not hold your hand through labour like we midwives do, and they may leave you to it and come back for the birth, but if you have gone private and paid for one, you will have built a beautiful trusting relationship with them and they will be so excited to meet your baby. Their knowledge of pregnancy and birth is profound and you will miss them once your pregnancy and birth are over. Your six-week check-up will

Ground zero: the birth

be something you look forward to, and your obstetrician will also be excited to see how much the little babe they monitored so closely in pregnancy for nine months has grown.

If you are birthing in the public system, there is no reason you will need to see an ob unless you had a complicated pregnancy, birth or emergency caesarean. More than likely you will get to stick with your gorgeous midwives instead.

I love my obstetrician, who has the patience of a saint. It might be the reason I have to keep going back for more babies, to see this compassionate, gentle man. Dealing with me as a midwife and pregnant mumma would have been no easy feat and he very kindly helped me without hesitation whenever I had a query (which was often, thanks to my irritable uterus). He was my go-to for everything pregnancy related, and this is exactly the relationship you should be able to have with your obstetrician.

The paediatrician

You are probably wondering what on earth a paediatrician has to do with your fourth trimester. Well, a lot if you have an unwell baby *or* if you have opted to have one check over your baby. These clever doctors are the bee's knees when it comes to ensuring our little ones are well enough to go home and face the big wide world.

Now, not everyone has a paediatrician. Not everyone wants to have one. Not everyone has to pay for one and some will never ever see one. If you have birthed your baby in the public sector, chances are you won't see a paediatrician unless your baby becomes unwell or has lost a significant amount of weight; or unless mumma has gestational diabetes or other complicating health factors. If you are private, it's the opposite. If you have a caesarean section (planned or emergency) there will be a paediatrician attending your child's birth, which you will have to pay for. They will generally visit you once or twice on the postnatal ward to ensure baby is well and everything is tracking accordingly in the world of newborns. If you birth vaginally in a private hospital and you have an uneventful (straightforward) labour and birth then a paediatrician is optional. I dare say most private patients decide to have their baby checked over by a paediatrician because when birthing 'privately', why not? But essentially if you do opt to see one, you have to pay for it.

If you birth publicly or privately and your baby has to go to the special care nursery or neonatal intensive care unit, your baby will be assigned a paediatrician to care for them while in hospital. The beauty of these baby-loving doctors? You can continue your baby's care with the same doctor outside of the hospital as they grow up. But this is also optional.

Ground zero: the birth

I have had a paediatrician care for all four of my babies post-birth. Alfie had a vacuum delivery (when a small cap is placed on bub's head to assist in the delivery) and as a result had a very big wonky head so was placed under a paediatrician's care. We were under a different paediatrician (whoever was on call at the time) with Essie because she was a breech (bottom-first) presentation up until twenty-four hours before birth, so we needed her hips checked and managed. Coco and Scout both needed a paediatrician as they were born 'flat', in other words they had a poor Apgar score due to the anxiety medication I was on. (An Apgar score is applied to babies immediately after birth to test certain health markers relating to heart rate, respiration, muscle tone, cough reflex and colour.) This was expected but nonetheless frightening at the time. Within a few minutes post-birth both of my babes were absolutely fine and feeding like champs skin-to-skin. One minute they were limp and slightly blue, and the next, after some oxygen, they were pink, feisty and raring for the boobie. Do you see why I love these doctors so much?

The physio
I wish physiotherapists got a bigger rap. I am talking a 'standing ovation, thanks for fixing my vagina' type of rap. The thing is, we often don't visit them enough,

---

Sore back post-birth? See a physio. Bulging lump in the fan? See a physio. Pissing your knickers? See a physio . . . Are you a mumma? See a physio.

Ground zero: the birth

and I am 100 per cent guilty of this. Sore back post-birth? See a physio. Bulging lump in the fan? See a physio. Pissing your knickers? See a physio. Weak core? See a physio. Birthed vaginally? See a physio. Birthed via caesarean? See a physio. Painful sex? See a physio. Hurts to poo? See a physio. Are you a mumma? See a physio. They are wonderful and clever and relatable and put us all back together again. God bless the physio for reassuring me my vag wasn't falling out and that it could all be fixed with some good posture and regular pelvic floor exercises. You can pay to see a physio privately or in many cases you can access their care and opinion via the public system post-birth. Either way, whether you feel like you require it or not, book an appointment with them. You cared for your body during your pregnancy and now it is time to give it a spring clean and service post-birth.

True story: after I had Essie – who was a super easy, gentle birth by the way – I was absolutely sure my insides were falling out of my vagina. The heaviness, the lag, the ... *errrr ummmmm* ... lump that was protruding that I had one million per cent catastrophised in my mind, was just a small, and I note *small*, prolapse that was fixed after one million pelvic floor exercises and taking it god damn easy. The poor physio would have been traumatised by my visit. In true Amelia form I carried on like a crazy

The Fourth Trimester

person, demanding she fix my broken vjj, but instead of running for hills, she gave me a cuddle and said, 'This will be back to normal in no time', and wasn't she right. You know when they give you the advice not to exercise too soon and carry heavy things like your toddler on your hip all day? Listen to them, they know their shit.

CHAPTER 2

The hours after the birth

I bet no one has spoken to you about the hours after birth. When it's over. It's all done and dusted. Your uterus soon to be completely empty. It's vacant again, and if it is to be occupied once more, it won't be for a long while. Adrenaline now runs your life and your brain is trying to catch up with what your body has just gone through. Your emotions are high. As high as the sky. Your heart has doubled in size and this euphoria runs deep into the night with your baby by your side. This time together – you, your baby and your partner – is a chance to rest, heal and breathe in all of the joy and love this experience has given you. You will never get these moments back.

They are precious and so fleeting. Once-in-a-lifetime-type stuff. Surrender wholeheartedly to this moment in time for as long as you can. If I could bottle the post-birth hours up, I would, a billion times over. Despite it being so important, remember this too shall pass, so do not rush the post-birth process one single bit.

Cutting the cord – delayed cord clamping

Have you heard about this? Fancy pancy delayed cord clamping? At one time people may have thought it was a passing 'trend' but I am here to tell you it's here to stay *babbbbyyyyy*, and for all the best reasons too! Delayed cord clamping has actually been around for a long time. The first research on it took place back in the 1940s, but it has really only become a household term in the last five or so years. Once upon a time, a baby was born, then placed onto mum's chest and the umbilical cord cut and clamped instantly. From that point on, the baby was fully separate from the placenta. In modern medicine we try to practice delayed cord clamping as much as possible as the benefits are plentiful. The American College of Obstetricians and Gynecologists lists the benefits, particularly in preterm births, as being associated

The hours after the birth

with the 'establishment of red blood cell volume', decreasing the potential need for blood transfusion, and also lowering the risk of nasty things such as your baby's gut tissue dying and bleeding on the brain. It also improves transitional circulation. For term babies that are healthy, delayed cord clamping is still recommended for a minimum of thirty seconds post-birth (acog.org) to improve iron stores and increase overall haemoglobin levels. Most births average around one minute of delayed cord clamping. The benefits for babies are just so damn good. Kind of like being born with their own little iron infusion that we as adults have to beg our doctors for. There is, though, a super fine line to delayed cord clamping. This can be discussed further with your care provider. Obviously, if baby is born unwell or compromised, clamping and cutting the cord as soon as possible is recommended. Another exception is those couples wishing to bank their cord blood.

Delayed cord clamping is also offered to babies born via caesarean section, which is awesome. We really have come a long way to give caesarean mummas the best births and outcomes possible for them and their little ones. About time too.

This time together – you, your baby and your partner – is a chance to rest, heal and breathe in all of the joy and love this experience has given you ... Surrender wholeheartedly to this moment.

The hours after the birth

Skin-to-skin – vaginal birth

The moment you have been waiting for after nine long months. It all happens in such a rush. One minute you are pushing with every ounce in your body to bring your baby earthside, then you blink and baby is mushed against your chest. If labour felt like an eternity, believe me this moment feels forever. And you will want it to stay that way. A never-ending moment in time. You will be shaking with adrenaline and joy. The overwhelm of what your body just did and having your baby in your arms is remarkable. Whatever outfit you wore during labour will now be up above your head as baby lies so peacefully skin-to-skin on your chest. A place where all is calm. A place where the sound of your heart is music to their ears. A place where they feel safest with the familiar smell of their mother. Just like a kitten lies snug with its mumma, so too does your newborn baby nestle with you, clever mumma.

Skin-to-skin isn't complicated. It is essentially your baby's bare skin against your bare skin. The benefits of skin-to-skin are plentiful. Not only does it naturally help regulate your baby's heart rate and settle their breathing, it also assists their body to adapt to extra-uterine life. Your first breastfeed will generally occur skin-to-skin as this stimulates baby's digestion and interest in feeding. The warmth skin-to-skin provides is pivotal in supporting baby to adapt to life outside of the womb, particularly those born early or of a smaller size, as it helps to regulate a baby's temperature. I always recommend babies born to mothers with gestational diabetes spend as much time skin-to-skin as possible as it increases body temperature, which can assist in regulating blood sugar levels. Skin-to-skin also exposes baby to its mother's bacteria, which acts as infection protection. Skin-to-skin has also been proven to benefit unwell babies in the special care unit post-birth. It can improve their oxygen saturations and calm them down, which overall helps settle any respiratory distress (if there is any) by reducing their stress hormone otherwise known as cortisol.

And the perks of skin-to-skin aren't just enjoyed by baby. The benefits for mumma are also remarkable. Skin-to-skin can calm down a stressed mother, particularly if she is feeling unwell post-birth or with the delivery of the placenta. Skin-to-skin sends beautiful lovey-dovey hormones to her brain, stimulating a release of oxytocin and kickstarts mumma's milk supply and breast-feeding. Skin-to-skin allows mum and bub time to bond and build chemistry with one another. For mums who lose more blood than is normal post-delivery, it can help to slow the bleeding as popping baby on the breast and feeding sends messages to the brain to produce hormones that

The hours after the birth

in turn naturally make the uterus contract, which is important in control of postpartum bleeding. All of this sounds like a fairytale, right? But I have to be honest, skin-to-skin isn't always possible, despite our best efforts as midwives to achieve it. If mumma isn't available for whatever reason and the other parent feels comfortable with the idea, the midwife can initiate skin-to-skin with them or with the support person. Sometimes when a baby is born they may not be able to achieve full skin-to-skin of any kind. Generally this is because a baby may come out struggling to breathe and establish respirations within the first few minutes post-birth. Babies born below optimal birth weight or much earlier than normal are also complicating factors in the postpartum period that may make skin-to-skin initially challenging. Sometimes too we have these wonderful labours and births and all of a sudden baby on the chest has gone a little quiet, which may necessitate whisking them away briefly for some assistance at the resuscitation cot. On occasion this does happen, unexpectedly, causing increased stress and anxiety for the new parents, not to mention baby. But thankfully, in this day and age we have excellent medical knowledge, specialists and equipment, which should see your baby only separated from you for a brief amount of time. During this period, rest assured, your baby will be in the best of hands.

Alfie and Essie both got loads of skin-to-skin with me post-birth. Coco and Scout needed some brief resuscitation, so our skin-to-skin was initially put on hold, but once they were well enough they spent a long time against my chest, sucking away for most of the time. I remember Coco was a little bit cold, so after we had a long time together, and I was busting for a shower, Ambrose tucked her into his t-shirt where she stayed super snug for the next hour. During my skin-to-skin, my babies always, always, always had their first poo, which was just delicious (not). Nothing like some black tar being mushed into my own faeces somehow smothered all over my stomach and chest. How glorious. Birth is beautiful. And messy. And sweet. And smelly. And *ahhh* lovely. Yes, definitely lovely.

Skin-to-skin – caesarean birth

There is a myth that only vaginal birthing mummas get skin-to-skin with their baby post–caesarean birth. I am here to tell you as a midwife in the twenty-first century that this is just not true. Back in the day, sure, skin-to-skin may have not have been the norm due to the belief that mum needed to recover from surgery and was not stable enough to hold baby. It was perhaps also often a case of there not being enough

The hours after the birth

staff at hand to assist with skin-to-skin. Nowadays, with an understanding of the benefits and importance of skin-to-skin, your midwife will do their best to give you both this contact post-birth as quickly as possible while you are still in the operating theatre.

Some paediatricians let mumma have skin-to-skin before they move bub away to clamp their cord, check them out, give their first vaccinations and vitamin K, and weigh them, which is *amazinggggggggg* but not all offer this. Whether you are birthing privately or publicly, speak up and let your midwife/paediatrician know that skin-to-skin is of the highest priority to you once bub is born. Sometimes, just like a vaginal birth bub, a baby may have to go immediately to the resuscitation cot for assistance, but if bub is born well, there is no reason there can't be immediate skin-to-skin. *If* your doctor or midwife takes baby to do their checks, weighing and needles (or for whatever the reason may be) before coming to you first, make sure you ask them to keep this time apart as brief as possible. In some hospitals, if you are lucky, you may be able to keep baby directly on your chest for the entire time you are in the operating theatre. This is rare *but* it can be done if your midwife has the time and theatre staff are happy to cooperate. It's important to note, though, that if they don't allow it and you have to separate from bub, it's likely to be due to a lack of staff to facilitate, or for the purpose of keeping things sterile when suturing, or perhaps for safety reasons, for instance if they need to move you to another bed. One thing is certain, though: once you are in recovery you will be allowed all the skin-to-skin in the world if you are both well. Ask your midwife to unwrap bub and place them under your gown for some beautiful skin-to-skin. By this stage, your baby will definitely be ready for a feed so try to use this time for some uninterrupted skin-to-skin and feeding.

In any birth, vaginal or caesarean section, if you are unable to do skin-to-skin or simply do not feel comfortable to, your partner or birth support person can absolutely do this for you if you ask for it to be facilitated. It is a beautiful time for your partner to have skin-to-skin if they are given the chance. If you are in no rush to dress baby post-birth and have had a blissful stretch of uninterrupted skin-to-skin, and babe has had their first feed, you can see if your partner would like some skin-to-skin with baby also. If I could bottle this feeling up for myself, baby muck and all, I would forever and ever and ever. There is simply nothing like it.

The hours after the birth

Bleeding

Did you know that after giving birth you will bleed vaginally for up to six weeks? *I know right!!!* If you have a caesarean section, the same goes ... how fun is the female body? Well, it is super clever actually. The reason we bleed postpartum is because our once cute, cosy little placenta that had blood vessels running between it and our uterus has now been disrupted and is bleeding freely. It takes a few weeks for these bad boys to settle down and relax. As the days go on, the bleeding should settle. Postpartum bleeding (also known as lochia) will start as fresh bright blood and over the course of a few days turn pink, then brown and beigy-cream coloured ... Your midwife will check in regularly post-birth in relation to your blood loss, but it is *super* important to advise them if you notice any big blood clots or you are saturating more than one pad per hour. The levels of blood loss in the weeks post-birth depend on many things, such as whether you are breastfeeding, being super mobile or exercising a lot, and whether you're just waking up in the morning or after a big nap. Very much like a normal period, the more we move the more we tend to bleed, and when we wake in the morning with a full bladder then wee, we tend to wipe and have a heavier flow. Same same really, except postpartum bleeding, if not in the normal range, can cause complications when not addressed. If you feel unwell at any stage, experience pain, funky odour down there or start gushing or bleeding super heavily again it is important to let your caregiver know asap. The last thing we want is an infection or to be stuck with some retained placenta or tissue inside our uterus. Don't worry, this is very unlikely to happen to you, but it doesn't hurt to stay alert.

Thankfully, my postpartum bleeding with all four babies was super minimal, but I did spot up until week six. Some days I thought it was done and dusted then *surpriseeeeeee*, it was back. Draining, to say the least, but oh well. The uterus has to do what a uterus has to do.

Stitches

Don't freak out. Just because I am writing about this topic does not mean you will necessarily require stitches post-birth. In fact, many birthing women come out unscathed, but others, like me after my first birth, can't avoid them. I needed a large snip (episiotomy) to get big boy Alfie out. I swear it sounds scarier than it is, though, because I would happily relive his birth and postpartum twenty times over. But, I mean, let's

---

The benefits of skin-to-skin are plentiful. Not only does it naturally help regulate your baby's heart rate and settle their breathing, it also assists their body to adapt to extrauterine life.

---

be real, we would rather stitches than a gaping hole, wouldn't we? And yes, it can be tender down there for a while, so my *favourite* advice post-birth if you are one of the lucky mummas to cop a stitch or ten down there is to make besties with vjj ice packs as well as Panadol and ibuprofen. Also, sitting on a rolled-up towel shaped like a doughnut can *really* help take the pressure and ache out of the downstairs region. Make sure you keep the area as clean and dry as possible and change your pad regularly. The last thing you want is a smelly little infection down there causing a nasty extra burn and sting. I am making childbirth seem so joyful, aren't I?

If you have had a caesarean section you too will have stitches or perhaps some staples to close your wound. Either way, super mumma, you will need to take it very easy. Ensure you look out for any signs of infection or wound breakdown and let your caregiver know if your wound is red, hot, smelly or painful, or starts oozing. These could indicate an infection in your wound and that is the last thing we want for you when you are trying to recover. Make sure your wound is thoroughly dry post-shower and if it has any leakage or oozing, keep it as dry and clean as you can until you seek further instruction from your caregiver. We mummas are very fortunate that most of the time, both vaginally and abdominally, our stitches heal without issue and

The hours after the birth

we enter the fourth trimester stronger than ever, like the super mummas we are.

When my vjj copped stitches after Alfie's birth, I actually didn't expect them to be so painful. Not getting the actual stitches (I didn't feel a thing thanks to the epi), but boy oh boy the healing part. *Woweeeeee*. Tender chicken central. Thank goodness I didn't need them with my other three kids. I could blame it on a stretchy fan but I am thanking my ob for this and taking bloody good care of my peri during birth. After Alfie's birth, once my stitches dissolved I honestly had no idea where they even were. Not a scar to be seen in the mirror. Perfect if I do say so myself.

After birth pains

These are just plain rude. As if your body hasn't been through enough in the last nine months, and now this?

Imagine latching your sweet baby to the breast and as they gently suckle away, you are gazing into their eyes, falling in love all over again, and *bam*, all of a sudden your uterus reminds you who is boss with some serious after birth pains. Thanks to the lovely oxytocin hormone that stimulates the milk ejection reflex, which in turn makes us contract and cramp. Honestly, they can take your breath away. Although super common, you're unlikely to get these with your first baby – they are more likely to occur in subsequent pregnancies, and believe me when I say this, the more babies you have, the more painful they get. By baby number four, I was hot on the call bell begging the midwife for some *strongggg* pain relief. A bit of Panadol and ibuprofen did the trick, along with a bloody hot heat pack. Your poor uterus gets a constant workout, trying to go back into its old hiding spot, out of the limelight where it belongs, all the while stopping you from haemorrhaging like a mofo. Bloody hard work on its part, which is why it hurts us so much. The key is to take an analgesic half an hour prior to a breastfeeding in order to give it a chance to kick and ensure you feel minimal pain when your uterus contracts mid-feed.

There is definitely some impressive science behind these naughty pains though! Google 'involution' – it explains a *lottttt*. But honestly, why do they happen? And why the fuck don't they mention them during many birthing classes? Oxytocin, our 'love hormone', plays a crucial role in childbirth and in your physical and mental postpartum recovery. It's released in large amounts during labour and childbirth to help the uterus contract, hopefully in turn dilating the cervix and birthing the baby. After birthing the baby, you will

The hours after the birth

then birth the placenta. Another *big* part of the process sometimes overlooked in birthing classes. After your baby is born, your body continues to release oxytocin, especially during breastfeeding. This hormone helps the uterus contract again (how good is it being female?) to stop us from haemorrhaging postpartum, but it doesn't bloody tickle.

After birth pains, while uncomfortable (*'ken oath*), are a sign that your body is working hard to heal and return to its pre-pregnant state. Embrace this time of recovery (if you can) and remember that it's only a temporary phase for the next few days. This is just more proof that us women have superpowers.

After I gave birth to Essie, I thought that I had another baby left inside me, the cramps were so painful. Then with Coco and her constant feeding, *woweeeee*, I didn't dare put her to the boob without my regime of pain meds. They helped *so* much and so did my heat pack. With Scout, the cramps were brutal for two days – so much so that I was absolutely certain I was in labour again – and then all of a sudden, gone. I cannot reiterate more strongly just how real these pains are, but we need to remember they're there for good reason – our uterus is just looking after us.

Crying

You bet ya your little bebe is going to cry. Maybe not a lot initially, but believe me, it will happen. But that's cool, cool, cool. They can't talk yet. So they just cry to tell you what they want.

> *Wahhh* = Feed me, I am beyond starving. Didn't you see my early feeding cues two minutes ago?
> *Wahhh* = I'm cold. Crank the god damn heater.
> *Wahhh* = Change my nappy. This mustard shit is burning my bum.
> *Wahhh* = Cuddle me. I miss your tummy.
> *Wahhh* = I'm tired a.f. Swaddle me and put me to bed.
> *Wahhh* = Aunt Gladys's perfume stinks, save me.
> *Wahhh* = This bath is fucking freezing. Dress me.
> *Wahhh* = I overfed on my strawberry milkshake, burp me.
> *Wahhh* = This car ride is bumpy as hell. Get me inside.
> *Wahhh* = This tag on my jumpsuit is annoying the shit out of me. Cut it off will you?
> *Wahhh* = Don't put me down mumma, I need you, I want you.

The hours after the birth

And there you have it. I've officially unlocked the secret to your baby's cries.

Sometimes, though, your baby might just cry a little bit more and a little bit harder. You will soon learn between their 'normal' cry and their 'help, I am in pain' cry. It is like a telepathic feeling parents have. We just know, you know? And if you don't at the start, if it takes a while to find your feet, I pinky promise we have all been there. If you get home and your baby is *superrrrr* unsettled and crying flat out and nothing you are trying is working, then always check with your GP to make sure nothing else is going on.

If you are a breastfeeding mumma, your boobies will generally work their magic during these bouts of crying, but I will explain more about this topic when I touch on the 'witching hour' in Chapter 8.

I am not kidding when I tell you that Alfie did not stop crying for the first twelve hours post-birth. His vacuum delivery must have given him a bad, bad headache. It broke my heart. Then he perked up and was happy as Larry until week three post-birth when his colic started. Fuck me dead. I swear he didn't stop crying from then until we went to sleep school when he was six months old. No one could ever settle him but me and that's not an exaggeration. When I look back now, I know it's because he was overfed (he put on just under one kilo in almost two weeks) and the most tired baby of them all. We were caught in a vicious cycle of feed, back to sleep, and feed when he cried. I couldn't stand the crying. It broke my heart and triggered some serious anxiety. His paediatrician took one look at him and said there was nothing wrong him, he was just so damn tired and so was I. 'Let's get you both to sleep school,' he told us. And from there, my life changed one trillion per cent for the better. Gosh, I could write a whole book just on his sleep and the billion benefits that came with it. I'll talk more about sleep school in Chapter 8 and sleep in general in Chapter 9. I learnt so much from sleep school about my baby and the importance of good quality, restorative sleep.

CHAPTER 3

The first twenty-four hours

www.whirlwind.newlife.babyheaven.mumhealing.com. That is all I can say about that. *Ha!* Blink and it's over. *So* much happens in the first twenty-four hours. *So, so much.* Feeds, visitors, healing, midwife checks, pain relief, rest, baby stares, lack of sleep, nourishing food, heart explosions... where do we start? It all begins with the first breastfeed. And then it continues with subsequent feeds. And more of them. And lots of them. And more. And it doesn't stop until the baby starts eating proper adult food around six months. In the first twenty-four hours, make the midwives your

Make the midwives your best friends. Buzz them for feeds. Buzz them for questions. They are there ... to support you and your baby at the beginning of your postpartum journey.

The first twenty-four hours

best friends. Buzz them for feeds. Buzz them for questions. They are there (despite being swamped with a big patient load) to support you and your baby at the beginning of your postpartum journey.

The first breastfeed

It's inevitable, right? It has been a long time coming. Your breasts have been preparing for it from the very beginning. Will it be easy? Maybe, but probably not. That's okay. Practice makes perfect, just like riding a bike, right? Even the most experienced boobies that have fed children before may struggle to feed the next one because *every* baby is different. And on that note, *every* boobie is different. Even your left boob from your right boob – that's right, different. So, let's start by not being hard on yourself or your baby. Not expecting too much. In fact eliminating that pressure from the get-go.

Let's start from the beginning when your baby is placed on your chest nudie rudie, bloodied and gooey but super cute and sweet and swollen. You can't believe it . . . your baby is probably warmer and heavier than you expected, yet so petite you feel like you could break them by moving them even slightly. Wrong. Your baby is *so* tough. Let's not forget, they have either just been pushed out from your vagina with a tight perineum squashing their head or pulled (probably by forceps) from your stomach into a cold environment and wrapped in a not-so-soft towel. They are tough. In fact, far more resilient than we give them credit for. You won't break them and you certainly won't drop them, not with your partner there anyway... try to enjoy this moment, soon it will feel like it was a million years ago.

So, babe is on your chest, listening to its mumma's heartbeat, waiting and watching and meeting and greeting its new environment. If you watch closely, your baby might start licking their lips... a subtle sign it is getting ready to feed. It may start mouthing for the breast or else straight out tell you it's time to feed with a cry, demanding its food be brought to the table. You know mumma, you know exactly what to do. Trust your instincts. You might be scared to do it, but you can do it, and if you can't initially, *please* ask your midwife for help. Post-birth, the longer the feed you give, the longer you can rest without interruption... but remember it is such early stages in your feeding journey that at the moment we are just trying to get bub acquainted with the boobie. If baby manages a feed, brilliant result. The importance of a first feed extends far beyond just giving them something to drink. It assists in stabilising their blood

The first twenty-four hours

sugar levels, their body temperature, their energy levels and your blood loss. (Correct – every time your baby suckles away, it sends messages to the brain that make your uterus contract, which stops you from having an increase in blood loss.) It still blows my mind that our bodies make all these super fancy hormones and send these cryptic messages that we can't see or hear... unbelievable.

So, what happens when baby doesn't latch? Or has just a one-second feed? Or comes off screaming and won't settle despite your best efforts to feed? You take a deep breath and you buzz your midwife for a plan. It could be a case of, 'not to worry, you can try again in an hour or so', or 'let me express you and see if I can give bub some of your colostrum in a syringe or cup', or, if you have a baby with a low blood sugar level (often the result of gestational diabetes), a top-up feed (generally formula) may be recommended for the moment. So sit tight, cuddle babe skin-to-skin, and sip on a sweet juice, because we all know your body needs some sugar after that marathon, and then see how the new hour unfolds.

On the topic of formula/bottle feeding, I cannot tell you how much the stigma of this kills my soul, let alone how it makes new mums feel. As a midwife and International Board Certified Lactation Consultant (IBCLC), if I could have every single baby breastfeeding and every mother happily doing so I would, but that's not realistic. Firstly, when women opt not to breastfeed from the get-go, it is generally for a good reason ... and that's the thing, their reason shouldn't be questioned ... hell, we shouldn't even delve into their reasoning. Of course we educate that breast is best, which we all know it is, *bla bla bla*, but some women, physically, mentally and emotionally, can't. I learned very early on in my midwifery career that a common reason women wish to bottle or formula feed from the start is due to previous experience of sexual harassment or rape. The trauma is too harrowing for them. Beyond that, any decision a mother makes is hopefully an informed one, so the questioning should end right there and the wider community needs to zip their lips and butt out. There are too many horror stories of midwives and nurses forcing breastfeeding onto women with an aversion to it, which then becomes so strong the mother ends up an absolute belittled mess, which is not a great start to any motherhood journey.

All in all, the world would be such a better place if we nurtured every mother and their decisions instead of competing with their idea of what motherhood should be and look like. A content baby and a physically, emotionally and mentally well mother should be the end goal prior to leaving hospital, end of story.

The first twenty-four hours

If you are a formula/bottle-feeding mumma reading this, soon to have your own baby, it's best to check with the hospital that you are birthing at to learn about their regulations regarding formula/bottle feeding. Some hospitals require you to bring your own equipment (bottles, steriliser, formula) and others provide it all.

My goodness, there is so much to the fourth trimester isn't there, and we are only just starting to scratch the surface.

One thing I would *reallllllllllly* like to elaborate on for the breastfeeding mumma is not to stress about how much milk baby is getting from your breast. Because guess what? We will never know how much. Ever. But we don't need to either because we have other ways of knowing how much bub is getting, such as the number of wet nappies baby has in a 24-hour period, how your breasts are feeling, how much weight baby is gaining, how content baby is and how hydrated your baby looks. You see, our breasts are super dooper clever at doing what they are meant to. Well, most of the time anyway. They work off a 'demand creates volume' kind of thing. Meaning the more you put your baby to the breast and feed, the more milk your body will continue to make and regulate. It is only now due to social media we have this obsession with checking the amount of millilitres going into our babies' bodies and, honestly, it is insanity. Talk about creating anxiety and fixation at its finest. What happened to just trusting the process and rolling with it? Oh, that's right, social media screwed this for us too, but you are smarter than that mumma and I know, I just know, you will absolutely dominate this whole feeding thing no matter what!!

I remember I was *so* excited to breastfeed Alfie after he was born. As a midwife, I was dying to know what this was like firsthand. After birth he spent so long on my chest looking and licking around but would not bloody attach to my boob. And my boobs were the *perfect* feeding boobs. Big nips to latch on to, already oozing with colostrum, but he was like *'nup screw this, my head hurts too much to suck* and we went around in circles for the next twelve hours trying to get him to have a good suck. Once he got it, though, he got it. He was a piranha and didn't let go until he was thirteen months old. My second born, Essie, the littlest of them all, weighing in at 3.1 kilograms exactly thirty-seven weeks on the dot, found the nip before I could even see if she was a boy or girl. I remember visitors coming in wanting to cuddle while I was in the birth suite and the second I tried to move her from the boob (I know, bad move midwife but she had already had a good hour of sucking!) she would screech until I put it back in her mouth. She fed beautifully from birth right up

The first twenty-four hours

until eighteen months of age. RIP boobs. Coco, she really took the piss out of night two (keep reading and you will learn more). She was so disgusted by the thought of a dummy being shoved in to her mouth to give me some respite from her feeding that her scream for more milk could be heard from the bottom level of the hospital. I actually thought something was wrong with her because all she did was feed, feed, feed. My poor nips were *ice*. I fed her until (*clears throat*) two and a half years of age. The only way I could wean her (she was so addicted to my boob that not even being pregnant with Scout did the trick) was ... wait for it ... drum roll ... Dijon mustard on my nips. You heard it here first. Anyway, defs don't recommend that to wean your baby. *Ha!* Scout, my fourth, was probably the least demanding in terms of breastfeeding. She could take it or leave it. We of course persevered and it wasn't until the end of my fourth trimester with her that I felt like we absolutely mastered breastfeeding, and she is my bloody fourth baby. It is unbelievable how different each baby is, right? Their different needs, wants, personalities, all come into play when it comes to feeding.

Baby's first weigh

After birth, your baby will be weighed for the first time. Don't forget to grab the camera and snap this moment. A few days later (generally between forty-eight to seventy-two hours) they are weighed once again to check they are maintaining their weight and ensure they are getting adequate nutrition. It is totally normal and acceptable for healthy babies to lose up to 10 per cent of their body weight because, let's be real, by this time a mother's milk is not quite in yet and baby will have finally pooed and urinated and lost some of their post-birth swelling. If their weight loss is greater than 10 per cent and baby is otherwise well with mumma's milk coming in, a feeding plan is often recommended. The next weigh-in will check that there is an increase in weight not another decrease. Sometimes we mums hold our breath knowing this weigh-in is approaching but, honestly, deep breathe and don't stress. Your midwife and/or paediatrician will work closely with you and bub if there is a significant weight loss or if baby is exceptionally slow to gain weight.

Baby will continue to be weighed regularly in the first few months of their life, and most get back to their birth weight two to three weeks post-birth. When you see your health nurse, they will weigh your baby at every appointment, as well as measuring their length and head circumference. This is when you will become familiar with the term 'centiles' and more than likely become fixated on these little stats as your baby grows. Can you believe there was a time when women didn't weigh and measure their babies' growth? They just kept on keepin' on. Gosh, how things have evolved.

I must say, as a midwife it's pretty fun to guestimate the size of the baby on the scales. Sometimes we are *wayyyy* off but a lot of the time we are pretty accurate.

First moment alone with baby

This was a real pinch me moment for me. Like, is that really my baby next to me? I remember looking over to the bassinet that lay beside my hospital bed and doing a weird ass 'Hello, I'm your mumma' to my baby. Of course, not being able to see a centimetre in front of himself, he just stared back at me, but I swear he was looking deep into my eyes. I was so excited to be alone with my baby. *Do I pick him up and cuddle him or do I just let him be?* I would walk into the bathroom at the hospital just so I could walk out again and be like, *Right, he is still here, he really is mine.* How weird is that? Pretty funny though, *ha*!

If you feel sick at the thought of being alone with

bub for the first time, you are the same as ninety-nine per cent of new mothers. (I was just a weirdo desperate for my visitors and partner to piss off for five minutes.) You don't need to freak. Certainly not while you are in the hospital, anyway – you have a call bell. Press it the second you freak the hell out and a midwife will come in and tell you everything is fine and your baby just has the hiccups. Think about it . . . what's the worst thing that can happen when you are alone with your baby? They cry? You feed them. They cry and you can't pick them up because you just had a caesarean? Press your buzzer again. It does get easier I swear.

I tell you what you should do when you are alone with baby for the first time: lie your butt in that bed with your feet elevated on a pillow or two, pour yourself a hot cuppa and shut your eyes for ten minutes. It is so bloody liberating. The strangest part? When you do get a moment of silence, you will place your hand on your belly thinking you can feel baby kick. It's at this time I swear reality hits properly for the first time that the nine months that was, is now over. If you are panic ridden being alone with baby and are anything but relaxed, and your midwife is too busy to run to your side, send me an insta DM and I'll do my best to entertain you while my four monkeys hang off my back. Then you will realise just how cathartic that moment to yourself really is.

I tell you what you should do
when you are alone with baby
for the first time: lie your butt
in that bed with your feet
elevated on a pillow.

The Fourth Trimester

Dressing baby post-birth

Nawwwww this part is always so damn cute. Especially in first-time parents. My god, the partner and their shaky gigantor hands against their little one's body is to die for. They take on average four days, six hours and fifty-seven minutes to dress their baby for the first time, and once they finish their first birthday has likely come and gone. True story. Though some partners power through the first dress, others insist on doing it ever-so-damn slowly and independently, or eye us across the room hoping we'll come and do it for them because they are certain they are going to break their little teeny baby's arms and legs. Not to mention the nappy that is back-to-front. Bless these beautiful parents. I wish we could always film these teeny tiny moments for them to keep forever and ever. The reality is that at that moment they feel like they are dressing a porcelain doll and in a few months' time they will do it with their eyes shut. My best tip is to watch the midwife do the first nappy and dressing demo. Of course if you feel confident enough jump on in and finish it off. What we don't realise as parents is that our babies' bodies are so much stronger than we think. We can't break them. Did you just witness them be born into this world? *Woahhhhhh!* They can tolerate some seriously big forceps and pulling. Little champions.

The first twenty-four hours

Now, in any hospital, no matter what season we are in (summer or winter), your baby will be 'cold' inside. So, it's simple: the first outfit post-birth is a onesie or singlet followed by a snug jumpsuit, a hat and a nice warm swaddle and blanket. Adapting to life outside the womb takes a little bit of time (which is why we *loveeeee* skin-to-skin as I have explained), so these layers are important to keep bub adequately heated. The exceptions to the rule are when you are breastfeeding – always unswaddle them so they wake and have an efficient feed, and when sleeping them in their bassinet always take their hats off to comply with safe sleeping. Safe sleeping starts at the very beginning and overheating bub is something we want to avoid.

Your first shower

This is *so* underrated. I mean, the fact that you are sitting under a hot shower washing away the blood, sweat and tears with a jelly belly *alone* for the first time in nine months is just crazy. You don't even realise at the time – it is your first shower alone . . . like, truly alone in so long. No baby in your tummy, just you, an independent woman, thinking *What the fuck has just happened?* while smirking to yourself in between perhaps shedding a tear here or there. A big splash of body wash under the armpits, a wash of the sweaty hair, and a shower hose shooting up the fan fan accompany the remnants of what has just gone on over the last twenty-four hours, supplying a big smack of reality in the face. When you turn that shower off, it's back to game on. Mum mode activated. You dry yourself with caution, still tender in places you didn't know existed, all the while mopping up the blood running down your leg from your vagina while quickly trying to insert a nappy into your undies to catch more before the towel turns completely red. You feel such a sigh of relief, being all clean and fresh, but also shaky and vulnerable. The shower was probably too hot, your shaky legs and body remind you so, you also acknowledge you haven't drunk anywhere near enough water in the last few hours, and trying to find the deodorant you swear you packed is proving to be a futile game of hide-and-seek. For a moment you remember you have a baby on the other side of the door, your very own baby, perhaps swaddled in your partner's arms, that is due for a second attempt at breastfeeding in the next hour, which leads you to question where the breast pads are before you open that door. *Stop*. I am telling you right now, no breast pads needed right now, just enjoy your itty-bitty titties before they turn into super melons over the next few days. Tuck your little belly into some serious granny undies, strap on a singlet and some comfy leggings or PJs, and there you have it, your first shower, all alone, before the real fun begins.

My first shower felt like a dream . . . *Did all of that really just happen? Did I just give birth to my first child? Did I really have a room full of visitors out there to meet this long-awaited arrival?* It was insane. My legs were super jelly. After a combined spinal/epidural anaesthesia and almost twelve-hour labour, it was nice to be able to stand up and stretch them. I vividly remember standing in the shower with the water pouring over my back after Alfie was born, looking at my blood going down the drain thinking *That's it, it's all over now* . . . I felt a little sad in that moment, that I now had to share him with the world, but little did I know, our time together was just beginning. The first shower really is a time to debrief with yourself for the first time. It is crazy what our bodies do. The tummy I was now washing was empty, all alone. I could pull my pants up without hesitation. I was sore though. Gosh I was sore. Everything ached. My heart a little, my tummy a lot, my legs and back even more. This time alone was needed. So necessary. So underrated.

Let this be a little note to you to really sit back (literally) and let that water pour over you as you breathe through what has just occurred. Enjoy it. Don't rush it. Sit with it. This really is the only moment for a long while that you will have all alone, to yourself. How did we ever take a solo shower so for granted? You will understand me after you have kids, I promise.

Baby's first bath

Everyone is always in such a rush to bathe their new baby. I get it. They are covered in all the birth muck – dry blood, poo, wee, sweat, vernix, fluid! But the truth is it is best to delay the first bath as long as possible. In our Western society, though, if we make it to twenty-four hours without a bath that is considered a win, *ha*! The thing is, a baby's skin is so precious. So fragile. So new. All that muck on their skin is a protective layer and nourishes their little bodies. We also delay bathing them straight after birth as they tend to drop their body temperature quite quickly and may struggle to stabilise it too soon after birth.

Personally, I waited twenty-four to forty-eight hours before bathing each of my babies as I love all that newborn freshness goo smell . . . it's heaven. Fun fact: Alfie had his first bath with Ambrose after we'd left hospital. I bathed Essie on my own in hospital. My mum and sister bathed Coco for the first time and Scout was bathed by one of my besties for her first time. How lucky I was to have such willing people to help. From their first bath, I have always made it a

The first twenty-four hours

ritual to bath my kids every night before bed. It is such a gentle, nice, relaxing way to head into the evening ahead, and I swear it is the reason my kids' witching hour is always short-lived.

Baby's first poo – meconium

No chance you have pooed yet mum – you generally won't for forty-eight hours post-birth – unless you nearly shit the bed like me due to my irritable bowel from all the wonder drugs. I am talking about baby's first poo! Yours comes later on . . . and gee whiz, isn't that a beautiful time once that bugger is out of your bum.

But the baby poo . . . the good old black tar, icky, sticky, meconium baby poo . . . be prepared guys, it is more than a sticky one and it may take a whole packet of baby wipes to scrape it off the butt, which is why I always recommend to my patients a bag of cotton balls instead dipped in some warm water – so much gentler on their fresh new butty-butt. Within the first twenty-four hours of life (hopefully not while in utero), your new baby should pass their first 'stool' known as meconium. It is dark, sometimes black looking but more often a super dark green *thick* paste, which is passed a few times until they begin to move onto

Baby poo is your new norm and now part of your everyday life.

The first twenty-four hours

transitional stools over the first few days post-birth. If you are one of the fortunate ones, your baby might shit all over your tummy and chest the moment they are born, or more than likely you will be greeted with it in the middle of the night and think *how the fuck did my baby just push that out?* Once you have nailed your first mec clean-up, the rest is history. The best part? Meconium doesn't smell!

Baby poo is your new norm and now a part of your everyday life so just embrace the thousand nappy changes you will be performing, *ha*! Who would have thought the start of your baby's digestion could be so interesting? Dark green poo to light green to yellow all within the first week of birth! The more milk your baby drinks the quicker the stools transition as their bowels clear out and adapt to their new kind of poo for the next six months or so until they commence solids. The midwives will also be checking babe has urinated so try to keep a basic record of what you see in their nappy every time you change it.

I was really blessed (eye roll) to have my babies do their very first-ever poo all over my chest. Each of my four kids opened the floodgates upon my belly and smothered me in it. I looked like a van Gogh painting gone way wrong. Green here, red there, brown to the side, white yellowy vernix mixed in. I was a fresh jelly cake of afterbirth, and what a delight it was.

I remember Ambrose changing Alfie in the middle of the first night and being like, *Milly, what the fuck is this?* ... pretty sure every partner has thought the same. Super effort to our little babies for managing to push this thick tar out in the first place, pretty impressive.

Your first poo

Who would think such a big deal would be made over your first poo? We midwives make it our priority that you back that beast out with comfort because we need to make sure you can manage this bodily function without any medical assistance before you head home. There would be nothing worse than going home post-birth only to need to return to hospital with a brick stuck up your butt, not to mention the tummy pains!

Post-birth, your midwife should ask daily if you have opened your bowels. If you haven't and they offer you an aperient (stool softener), please for the love of god take it. Trust me. All the analgesia you take post-birth can easily clog you up, and especially if you have had an episiotomy or tear, or have haemorrhoids, a stool softener is given so you don't strain your butthole further or open your perineal tear from pushing too hard. Sounds delightful, doesn't it? It is also really

The first twenty-four hours

important to avoid straining in order to support your pelvic floor. Once you do poo, though, you will feel like a new woman.

Not counting shitting myself in bed post-birth with Alfie, my most memorable post-birth poo occurred once I got home. I remember having a log stuck so hard in my butt I spent over an hour in the toilet trying to weasel it out the best I could. I cried. I sent Ambrose to the chemist then I shoved a laxative as far up my bum as I could, because that constipation pain was worse than childbirth, I am not for one second kidding you. Trying to back one out with a fanny full of stitches was pure torture. Thank god that rock finally dislodged from my butt because I thought my bum was going to split in two. It is safe to say I made sure my bowels were as slippery as the slopes with my subsequent kids. I never ever wanted to experience that again. Let this be your warning to get on the good stuff early on. Prune and pear juice may be sickly sweet but your bum and tum will appreciate it.

The first night

My first night after giving birth to Alfie was full of pain from an aching vagina thanks to my episiotomy, mad dashes to the toilet before I pooed my pants

The Fourth Trimester

thanks to the million drugs in my body, *ha*, and a baby who cried the *whole* night because his head was so sore from the vacuum that assisted in birthing him. Ambrose slept on the couch snoring his head off, only to wake every hour to come and kiss his new baby and me while desperately trying to get Alfie to feed because surely a boob could soothe his pain. Of course, eventually, the baby settled and then *BAM*, my adrenaline was so sky high I couldn't fall asleep. So instead I took a million more photos of my baby, shoved some more boob in his mouth, weed once more, then finally shut my eyes. Before I knew it, the midwife entered for 6 am observations. Nothing like a fundal check (rub of the uterus), some analgesics and a check of the vagina before brekkie to make sure all was looking right. I didn't care about the lack of sleep though . . . I was so excited to show my family and friends my greatest achievement that hobbling around the room with a swollen butthole and vjj was the least of my worries. Sleep . . . who needs it, right? I was a god damn super woman after a twelve-hour labour and a sleepless night on top of it. I felt like I was walking on cloud nine.

My first night after giving birth to my second, Essie, twenty months after Alfie, I sprang out of bed with an intact vagina and minimal bleeding. I felt a billion dollars . . . suffice to say my second birth was

The first twenty-four hours

much smoother than my first . . . and, to be honest, I would say that is the case in 99 per cent of second births.

My first night with bub in my subsequent pregnancies looked so different to when it was just Ambrose, Alfie and me. When I had Essie I spent the first night alone with her while Ambrose wrangled Alfie the mumma's boy at home. I felt so weird without him there. Alfie that is. I was so used to giving him my all that when Essie came along, I was in for a rude awakening how much my heart would hurt leaving him 'properly' for the first time. While he was in good hands without his mumma, it's hard to shake that feeling of guilt for leaving your other baby at home.

I feel like the more postpartums we experience, the more tiring they get. Maybe it's because we are older with each new postpartum experience, or perhaps it's because we are already exhausted from caring for our other children. The key to surviving each time is to rest any spare second you get. By my third baby, Coco, I was absolutely pumped for a hospital staycay. Alfie and Essie were that bit older and so much more independent that the guilt of parting with them was more like a celebration of time to myself with my new little sidekick. Come baby number four, I told Ambrose they could only visit once (as if this happened) because I wanted the four days to myself to recover and 'bond' with my new baby girl. I am pleased to say Ambrose was first in the hospital door with three kids in tow, ready to share my hospital breakfast with me after his 'exhausting' night of sleeping through with three older kids. I think parents of multiple kids will get this need to have time to yourself before bringing babe home to the amazon jungle of feral hyenas and stray cats.

Needless to say, my first night alone after birth with all my babies was pure bliss. Cups of tea, biscuits I didn't have to share with anyone and a million baby snugs and kisses. Heaven.

CHAPTER 4

Feeding

Feeding! This would have to be hands down the hardest part of having a baby. Perhaps there should be a whole antenatal class dedicated to this. I am super lucky. Apart from stingy, shredded nips for a few days I had a fairly seamless feeding journey, but I'm well aware that not every mother is the same. *Thankfully* these days there are so many ways to feed your baby, ensuring they are getting adequate nutrition and hydration. We are all well aware that breast is best; however, we also know that not every mother can successfully breastfeed or in fact wants to breastfeed, for various reasons. Manufacturing has come a long way to assist breastfeeding mothers, with the modern

---

Our milk production is
bloody fascinating and so god
damn clever that it changes
according to our babies'
demands, needs and wants.

---

design of wireless hospital-grade breast pumps and devices such as nipple shields to protect our sore little nips. For those not wanting to breastfeed full stop, we also have the option of clean, nutritious formula that is readily available to purchase, and appropriate bottles that can be easily sterilised. Whichever way you choose to feed your baby, you are everything your baby needs and a wonderful, wonderful mother. It is important that I do make mention, though, just how clever our damn bodies are when it comes to intuitively feeding our babies.

Stages of breastmilk

Did you know that your breasts are so clever that they go through different stages of milk production in order to produce sufficient milk for your baby? They know our babies' guts can't tolerate a big dose of milk on day one of life, so they start with some itty-bitty colostrum, which then turns into transitional milk before we produce high-quality mature milk for our bubs as they grow over the first few weeks of life. Crazy huh?

Our breastmilk provides everything our teeny babies need to survive and thrive from birth. Our milk production is bloody fascinating and so god damn clever that it changes according to our babies' demands, needs and wants. The stages of breastmilk production go something like this:

Colostrum: Liquid gold

Absolutely no doubt about it, you will have heard of the good old 'colostrum' that has been around since the first woman ever conceived (*Hi, Eve*). The pregnant body starts producing colostrum around week twelve to eighteen (no one is 100 per cent certain) and even though we don't necessarily see it that early, lo and behold it's stored away in our breasts ready to meet our baby in months to come. This liquid gold is the first milk your baby will receive if breastfeeding and is loaded with the richest vitamins and nutrients, all with incredible benefits for your new little bub.

Colostrum is thick, sticky and mega-concentrated as it is packed with antibodies and nutrients that are essential for your newborn baby to thrive. It is easy for their tiny tummies to digest and helps to kickstart their digestive system, acting as a gentle laxative to help clear out the meconium, the first stool, which is *veryyyyy* thick and gooey. Colostrum can range from being clear in colour to a deep yellow, to almost orange for some women. No matter the colour or how much colostrum baby actually receives, every single drop is extremely powerful.

If your baby is struggling to attach to your breast

or unable to breastfeed because they are separated from mumma (for example, if bub is in the special care nursery – touch wood not the case), expressing this liquid gold will be recommended by your midwife. They will be able to assist you in doing so as well.

Transitional milk: The changeover

Transitional milk comes into play on approximately day three to five post-birth. You will notice your small drops of colostrum have now transitioned into bigger quantities of milk and may have also changed in colour and consistency. This is your transitional milk – the in-between goodness of your colostrum and mature milk. Your boobies generally feel fuller, look bigger (*hey, Pammy Anderson*) and you will be able to hear your baby audibly swallowing. Your baby will also be much more content once the transitional milk hits the good spot. Baby won't have to work super hard for it either, but be assured, regular, demand feeding is what keeps this precious milk flowing in abundance and maturing each and every feed.

Like colostrum, transitional milk provides high levels of antibodies, while increasing in calories, fat, and lactose to meet your baby's growing belly and needs. During this phase, you *might* experience what's often referred to as 'engorgement', where your breasts feel quite full and firm. *Do not fret if you don't.* You still have a brilliant supply, I promise. Frequent feeding can help manage this fullness, along with heat packs on your breasts prior to a feed and ice packs after a feed to keep your milk flowing smoothly while decreasing inflammation that is engorgement. You might also notice your body temp spike a little and a hot flush here and there. This is generally nothing to worry about and just another sign your milk is well and truly 'coming in'.

Mature milk: The perfect balance

When your bub is around two weeks of age, your breastmilk transitions to what we call 'mature milk'. This is the milk your baby will continue to drink until the end of your breastfeeding journey. Mature milk has two main parts: foremilk and hindmilk. Both have amazing benefits.

Foremilk is the milk your baby gets at the beginning of a feeding. It's lighter, more watery, and packed with lactose and proteins to quench their thirst. Let's say it's like the 'entrée' to their dinner.

Hindmilk comes later in the feeding and is richer and creamier, loaded with fats that help your baby gain weight and feel satisfied. The hindmilk is what keeps your bub fuller for longer and is loaded with calories. It is the 'main' meal served at dinnertime and is perfectly balanced alongside the foremilk to provide

Feeding

all the essential nutrients, antibodies and hydration your baby needs for each feed.

Mature milk adapts to your baby's growth and demands, even so cleverly altering its milk composition during every breastfeed. Also – if your baby ever becomes unwell, your breasts often become aware before you do, naturally changing the milk composition to try to 'fix' baby and give them an extra immune boost. This is all performed when your baby's saliva touches your breast. Are you mind blown by this? I absolutely am!! *Insane*.

I could harp on about breastfeeding and its billion benefits forever. One of the most beautiful aspects of breastfeeding is how your body intuitively knows what your baby needs at each stage. From colostrum to transitional milk to mature milk, every drop is designed to suit your baby's growing needs and that is just so beyond me. Unbelievable.

While I feel passionately about breastfeeding, it's not lost on me that not everyone has a successful journey, finds it natural at all or even chooses to feed this way to begin with. Remember, breastfeeding is a journey for both you and your baby, and while natural and beneficial, I am mindful it is not for everyone for their own personal reasons.

Breastfeeding takes time, patience, and *lots* of practice. Trust in your body's wisdom, seek support when you need it, and cherish these moments of closeness and nourishment with your little one. Soon they will be preferring a hot cross bun to your breastmilk.

The milk is in – holy cow udders!

Yep. You best believe it. Those boobies that once resembled pancake bubbles now mimic hardcore coconuts and are super sweet to your baby too! You might be in agony with your new set of boobies or you may be loving the upgrade to full, upright ones, but either way, I promise they settle. Eventually. With the help of your baby and the regulation of your milk production. Clever things our boobies are. So, when does the milk officially 'come in', you ask. Well, how long is a piece of string? Milk generally transitions from colostrum to mature milk between day two to five. I tend to go with the latter because usually by day five women go *Woah ... would you look at my rock hard boobs*, whereas on day two they have usually only grown slightly (though women assume that's the milk). Don't get me wrong, it could have transitioned that quickly, but it's rare, especially in first time mothers. And then there are the other mummas whose milk takes a little longer and that is totally okay too!!! It can be super stressful and frustrating for you, especially if you

Feeding

have a baby squawking at you for more, more, more but there are ways around this and things to assist in pushing your milk along to grow up and mature quicker than it would like.

The key to breastfeeding is to have skin-to-skin from birth, and to feed, feed, feed as much as your baby will take it and your boobies can handle it ... the more you feed, the more you make and the quicker it comes. This is where the whole supply = demand thing comes into play. Kind of like riding a bike ... we start off slow and steady ... the more we practice the stronger and bigger our calf muscles get ... if we keep riding marathons, we get better ... if we slow down, our riding muscles get smaller and we lose motivation. Our breasts are very much the same. The more we feed the bigger they become and the more plentiful the supply; the less we feed, the smaller they become and the less supply. More to come on your feeding journey ahead, but for now, support those boobies, feed that gorgeous baby and enjoy the start of nurturing your child.

With my first baby Alfie, my breasts were honestly out of this world enormous by day three. They were hot, engorged, full and very tender. With Essie I didn't notice such an obvious transformation. They grew, but nothing like they did when I had Alfie. They still had plenty of milk initially, but looking back now I can definitely see that feeding Essie I had the smallest

One of the most beautiful aspects of breastfeeding is how your body intuitively knows what your baby needs at each stage.

Feeding

supply out of all my babies. I really think the stress of two under two played a big part in this, but she wasn't a needy baby, so she just went with the flow. With Coco it was almost four years between pregnancies, so I felt like my boobs had had a good break. By the time my milk was in they were absolutely horrifically big. I also had a huge oversupply even though my milk took a good four days to come in. With Scout, it had really only been six months between breastfeeding so, sure, they grew slightly bigger when my milk came in, but they were like well-used socks by this stage. Scout was my only baby to lose up to 10 per cent weight, but I attribute this to her not being a very efficient feeder in the first week or two. You really can't compare apples to oranges. Every baby is different and so is each feeding journey. Whichever baby you are at, I hope you have an easy, rewarding feeding journey ahead.

Breast care

There is no denying that when you breastfeed, particularly for the first time, your breasts and nipples can cop a beating but we *realllllly* want to avoid damage from the get-go. I would be lying if I said they won't be tender in the early days, especially the first few days and when your milk comes in. I mean, can you imagine your breasts not feeling uncomfortable when their volume increases and you have tender nipples being sucked? Rest assured, there are many things you can do to minimise nipple damage and pain in the early days to help ensure your breastfeeding journey ahead is a beautiful and enjoyable one.

It starts with letting the midwife assist you with your first feed. If you can get a good latch, this will greatly decrease nipple damage. Easier said than done, I am well aware. I have been there four times, *ha*, but if you can gently guide your little babe in the right direction of a good latch and support them well, they will be able to find the breast and nipple and feed efficiently early on. Our babies are far more clever then we give them credit for and they have an innate ability to feed like champions if we let them. This is why I always suggest utilising your midwife as much as you can in the hospital for breastfeeding assistance until you are left to pave the way at home, essentially by yourself. Don't worry, you too mumma are *very* smart and will soon learn how to feed your baby and what feels right compared to what doesn't.

Sometimes, despite the perfect latch, your nipples may still be super tender and that is okay. I mean, it's not really but it will be okay. First up, if they are obviously shredded, damaged or bleeding you can use many over-the-counter creams, lotions and potions to

Feeding

help with healing your nipples, but the best thing you can do is to seek the support of a lactation consultant *and* pack some Cosy Nips (silver goodness to protect your feeding nipples) to your hospital bag prior to delivery. These bad boys made of silver have the most phenomenal healing properties and work all kinds of magic on the nips, but you need to make sure you do not have a shallow or poor latch causing the damage, because they won't get better until you fix the problem. Sometimes, resting your breasts and nipples is vital to heal.

Breast pain is a separate issue to nipple pain and could be the result of your milk coming in and your breasts expanding, or it could be engorgement, or, *touch wood (not)*, mastitis . . . but that is very unlikely in the first few days post-birth. Some pain is normal when baby latches on and starts suckling, so for the first thirty seconds or so it's deep breathing while your baby begins, but then it should subside. If it doesn't and your breastfeeding continues to be painful and unenjoyable, please know there is plenty of help out there so book in with a lactation consultant as soon as possible.

The treatment recommended for engorgement is heat packs prior to a breastfeed and ice packs after. Both help with inflammation and making your breasts more comfortable between feeds. For suspected mastitis (god forbid) you will need a medical review and possibly antibiotics. All these issues can be addressed with the help of a good midwife or lactation consultant.

Even if you face some early breastfeeding challenges, it does not mean your entire journey will be like this. And it is important to note that some women will never have any breastfeeding issues, whereas others might face challenges along the way. It's all a part of the journey I say.

Breastfeeding challenges

As I've mentioned previously, initially sorting your breastfeeding latch is important to reduce the pain a feed can cause, but what about other challenges a breastfeeding mother can face? I swear if every mother was assigned their own breastfeeding consultant at home, we would have close to a 100 per cent success rate. Sometimes, a mother's breastfeeding journey can have a few hurdles along the way, such as a low milk supply, oversupply, no supply, hypoplastic breasts (too much glandular tissue making it impossible to create adequate milk), nipple vasospasm (constricted or tight blood vessels), nipple/breast thrush, inverted or flat nipples, tongue tie or if baby has intolerances to things

---

Even if you face some early breastfeeding challenges, it does not mean your entire journey will be like this.

---

in a mother's diet. The list goes on and on, but I swear the benefits of breastfeeding outweigh the negatives most of the time, apart from when a mother's physical or psychological health is affected, or baby is not thriving as they should be. All that being said, seeing your GP, lactation consultant or Maternal and Child Health nurse can be a mammoth help and I absolutely encourage this to ensure your hurdles are overcome as quickly as possible.

It is not all doom and gloom, as I have said, and I definitely don't mean to put a dampener on the idea of breastfeeding for you, but I think a reality check can sometimes work in more positive ways, particularly so that you are well prepared and equipped for any challenges if and when they arise. Take each breastfeed as your chance to put your feet up, rest, hydrate, connect with your baby, replenish yourself and have your baby to yourself. My mother always said that if she hadn't breastfed her five babies, she would never have sat down during the day. How true this is.

The bottle-feeding mumma

I want you to know that *you* are just as important as a breastfeeding mumma. A bottle-feeding mumma has a few options when it comes to choosing how to feed

Feeding

their baby: formula feeding only, mixed feeding or expressed breastmilk given exclusively via the bottle. Many mothers for various reasons opt to bottle or formula feed from the get-go and that is totally fine. Other women are desperate to exclusively breastfeed but have a genuinely low supply and despite their best efforts to increase it, have no choice but to top up with formula or breastmilk. And then there are some mums who cannot breastfeed full stop or don't wish to but are happy to feed their breastmilk exclusively via a bottle. The reasons for bottle feeding are endless. Some mothers need to protect their mental health and find that mixed feeding or exclusively bottle feeding is best for them and their baby. Some babies are born with disabilities and a special bottle is the only way they can take in fluid. Some babies have major intolerances and allergies, making breastfeeding challenging for mum and baby. Some mothers simply want to bottle feed and that is the end of their story. Whatever the situation, I wish the world would stop propagating the bottle-feeding stigma and people would keep their assumptions to themselves.

I remember someone asking why I was so desperate for Alfie to take a bottle at one point. I cried and cried because I was so exhausted, not to mention physically depleted, and this was not the judgemental comment I needed. And to make it worse? He refused the bottle.

And I mean zip shut lips, nine different types of bottles, four different hands, dark room tricks and nothing bloody worked. With Essie I knew she simply had to love the bot bot (as well as my boob) because I was still working on maternity leave (what leave?) and needed to do home consults. She had to become au fait with the bottle. And thankfully she did. We breastfed 99 per cent of the time, but knowing she took the bot bot when needed was a breath of fresh air. Coco – forget it. The bottle was for the weak until she hit almost one. Scout loves a bot bot. I believe having the bottle as an option if needed has been why I have successfully breastfed for so long. And let me tell you one thing: bottle feeding is not the easy way out. Those plastic things are buggers to sterilise, store and fill!! Not to mention the cost of formula on top of buying all that gear, if you aren't going to pump and use your own milk. Kudos to these mummas getting woken in the night then having to scramble in the kitchen to make a bottle. That is time-consuming and hard work, so well done.

Pumping

For some reason, this generation (my generation) has an obsession with pumping. It wasn't so much of a

Feeding

thing back in the day, when you just put your baby to the breast if they were hungry and that was it. There is one big difference now, however: many mummas have to return to work much earlier than they used to. That means there is a higher demand to pump so that women can continue their breastfeeding journey despite work commitments. But what I don't quite get is the mummas that pump their tatas just to learn how much their baby is getting from the breast. Dear lord. If you are reading this and you haven't had your baby yet, for the love of god, don't do this. For your sanity. Honestly, save yourself.

Pumping is brilliant for mums returning to work; for babies with low birth weight or slow weight gain needing top-ups; to enable you to have a break or if you need someone to assist feeding babe; or if you have a low supply and are trying to encourage your milk production. Pumping can also help if you have damaged nipples or mastitis and are unable to feed. The benefits of pumping for these scenarios are *that good* and necessary that I even created my own wireless, portable, discreet breast pumps, and you bet my main clientele are mummas in the workforce, mummas with premature babies and busy mums on the run.

My ten best tips for pumping are:

The Fourth Trimester

1) Only pump if you need to; don't do it simply for fun as your breasts have a mind of their own and might overproduce, risking mastitis.
2) Make sure you get a pump that is hospital grade (mine is exactly this).
3) Fit yourself for the right flange size, otherwise you will struggle to drain the milk from the breast and also risk damaging your nipples and breasts.
4) Get a double pump if you intend to use it regularly.
5) Sterilising is so much easier than you think – no fancy equipment is needed at all.
6) Pumps are actually a great investment as you can use them for subsequent babies.
7) Put a pump on your baby shower list.
8) Pump in front of your child or while feeding from the other breast. If this isn't possible, scroll your phone looking at photos of your bub – this helps with your milk ejection reflex (let down).
9) Don't overpump if you don't have to.
10) If you want to solely pump and not breastfeed at all, I recommend pumping regularly two to three hourly until your milk is in, and then initially three hourly during the day and three to four hourly overnight. This will ensure your supply keeps flowing and producing adequately.

Rest assured I know many mummas who were unable to breastfeed successfully and went on to pump exclusively for their baby with no trouble at all. Another handy hint from me – a lactation consultant can be a wonderful addition to your pumping journey!

We have come ahead in leaps and bounds in the world of breastfeeding, believe me!

Bottle feeding and long sleep blocks

There is a commonly held assumption that if you breastfeed your baby instead of formula feed, there is no way your baby will sleep as well or be able to have longer blocks between feeds. I am here to tell you this is one big crock of shit. I mean sure, you will have friends with formula-fed babies who 'slept through' from week two, and then others that wake every two hours overnight. You will also have some breastfed babies that sleep through and give their mumma four-hourly feeds during the day. The reality is every single baby is different. Breast or bottle fed does not make a difference in terms of sleep. Sure, formula-fed babies take longer to digest their feeds compared to breastfed, which means they may not require feeds as often, but breastfed babies naturally get these brilliant sleepy hormones in their night feeds that keep them asleep longer than their baby friends who might smash 100 millilitres of formula at one week of age.

The pressure to achieve blissful sleep for our babies is real. All we really need to know is that whether your baby is breastfed or formula fed, they both need regular feeds day and night and will both 'sleep through' at some point in time. Should you 'top up' your baby with some formula to get a longer block of sleep at night? There is no need. I mean sure, you can if you wish, but honestly it's not necessary. The exception to this is if your paediatrician, midwife, lactation consultant or health nurse has recommended it for your baby, then of course it is best to follow their advice. Otherwise, I would encourage you instead to spend your time setting a gentle night routine consisting of a bath and feed at the same time each evening. I know this will give you and your baby a better sleep than worrying about how many millilitres of milk are in your baby's stomach.

We new mums just have to be mindful not to expect too much in the first few weeks and realise that this time together with our new bub is best spent loving each other sick, establishing feeding (bottle or breast) and milking all our visitors of the home-cooked meals that they have dropped off. I think the best way to prepare for sleep deprivation is accepting

---

We new mums just have to be mindful not to expect too much in the first few weeks.

---

it is normal for your baby to wake every two to four hours overnight for the first month or two. After that, you should increasingly see more three-hourly blocks of sleep overnight. Some babies are capable of longer blocks and that is perfectly fine if there are no concerns regarding their weight and mum's milk supply.

From around week three to five all my babies gave me a super long chunk of sleep at the beginning of the night (until the four-month regression, which I discuss in detail at the end of Chapter 9), which I believe was due to them getting a lot of daytime calories with plenty of day breastfeeds, and also by having a simple wind-down routine of an evening before bedtime. Some babies are true unicorns and sleep well from the get-go whereas others need some coercing to sleep longer blocks. Either way, remember your baby is not a robot and during the fourth trimester it is all about bonding and learning everything you can about your new baby rather than expecting them to adopt certain prescribed patterns of sleep as soon as possible.

CHAPTER 5

The (very) early days

The very early days post-birth consist of learning to feed your new baby, bonding with them, getting to know them and them getting to know you, and taking the time to rest in order to heal your body, mind and soul as much as possible. People, aka our family and visitors, tend to be naturally hyper-focused on the new arrival, and forget (unintentionally) just how much we, as mothers, need attention also. We have just birthed a baby and we are now tired. We are excited but exhausted. And we need the visitors, the family, the friends, the support network to do just that, support us. To be our village, like in the old days. Not to just hold the baby, but hold us too. Cook for us, clean for us, send us food hampers, take our other kids off our hands, and, also, give us space. While we love our visitors, family and friends, indeed we need them, we also need time to be just us, a new family unit.

Visitors in hospital

Ahhhhhh the excitement of meeting your new baby is next level. Be prepared for an avalanche of visitors that will soon break your hospital door down demanding cuddles, photos and more cuddles. They will want your birth story, your soul and your baby. Most are respectful . . . well, you would hope so. And others, not so much. Most women and their partners love the attention. Some pull us midwives aside and ask us to make excuses to eradicate the many visitors from the room and allow mumma and her baby to come up for air and catch their breath. Some request complete privacy from family and don't disclose that baby was even born until they arrive home. Some will be FaceTiming in the middle of their caesarean to help welcome their baby into the world. Some have several support people in the room cheering mum on as she births her baby. Some will have a room full of visitors waiting for her. Some will just want their other kids in for the first visit. Some request no visitors until the next day. Some don't have family or friends around at all. Some do it alone. All of it. Some don't have a choice. Some don't have grandparents or sisters or brothers or family to assist in the aftermath that is the fourth trimester, and others are so suffocated they don't want to leave hospital knowing what awaits them at home. Many families choose to have all their visitors attend the hospital so they can have some respite once they arrive home, and others do the opposite and use their hospital stay as rest, knowing chaos awaits them at home. What I have learned is that every birthing couple is different.

Whichever it is, whichever patient you are, please know this, from a midwife and mother: your body has been through far more then you realise. Your baby has endured a lot in the last twenty-four hours. Your baby just wants mum. Your baby needs good feeds. You, the mother, need to rest and restore. Your partner also needs downtime and TLC. Your visitors are great, and appreciated, and I do encourage them to a degree, *but*, and there is a big *but*, listen to your body. Respect your baby. *Use* this time in hospital to do nothing but heal and bond with your baby. You will never get this time back. Even if you are in a shared public hospital room, take this opportunity to have some downtime.

I wish I had taken my own advice. When Alfie

was born I had Ambrose, my mum, my sister and mother-in-law by my side. In hindsight that sounds ridiculous, but we were so excited, I wanted to share the moment with everyone, so I had them all. Once I was sutured post-birth, my other three siblings came in along with my dad, Ambrose's dad, my nephew and my three best friends. Yes, we are a crazy baby family. Ambrose is one of seven kids and I am one of five, so we knew our visitor numbers were going to be crazy.

For Essie's birth it was not as manic – the beauty of having a 7.30 am birth. And Coco was born during COVID so I had just three visitors in the hospital, which was actually *amazingggggggg* as I needed that downtime without even realising it. With Scout, baby number four, the visitors trickled in and out but most kept their visits for home time.

The time after each birth is *so, so, so* precious. The more kids you have, the more you have to share yourself between your baby and others, so for me, I found keeping visitors to a minimum in hospital this time around was a super smart decision. Not only did it give me a little more breathing space with my new baby, it also allowed my body some time to recover.

The (very) early days

Neonatal intensive care unit

The truth is, not everyone gets to experience the typical postnatal 'rooming in' with bub. Some little babes might have to go off to the special care nursery or neonatal intensive care unit post-birth. If you are separated from bub because they are unwell or need some extra care, be reassured that this time apart is generally only temporary and is usually short-lived. Bub will hopefully be well enough for some skin-to-skin under supervision, but if not, you can still spend lots of time bonding with them by their bedside and possibly even help care for them until they are in better health. If you are breastfeeding, then expressing regularly is super important so you can initiate your supply and maintain it. Before you know it, bub will be suckling away at the boobie and you will be in disbelief at just how quickly your little resilient one has made their way back to you.

If you have a bub that can't be with you immediately after birth, rest assured that the nurses and midwives will do their best to ensure you are both bonding and getting some special time together. The beautiful nurses and midwives that care for our sick little ones are real angels on earth. They truly give them 100 per cent care at all times, so please know that if this is your bub needing some assistance, they are in the best of hands. Before you know it, you will be back rooming in with your bub and will get to finally enjoy your postnatal experience together, despite it originally looking a little different.

Night two – the clusterfeed

You are now super tired, still in disbelief that the baby next to you is yours. You pull the cot beside you and fix your eyes on your baby. *Did this really happen? Is this baby really mine? Is it alive? Should I feed it?* The questions continue between a million smiles upon your face. In the moments of silence you will hear call bells going off, babies crying, mothers shooshing, conversations full of celebration and perhaps some tears in between. Your partner may have gone home for the night or, if you are one of the lucky ones, they get to stay with you both. Either way, one thing is for sure, you are getting more exhausted, ready to switch off for the night and hit the snooze button, *but* your baby has other plans. They are waking up properly for the first time since birth because, guess what, *they are now hungry*!! *Yayyyyy* . . . well, kind of *yayyyyy*. All of a sudden you have a baby that cries unless glued to your tit suckling away, and this is where they stay for the next twelve or so hours at least. They suckle, they fall

The (very) early days

asleep, they cry, they suckle again, they fall asleep... you quietly remove them and try to swaddle them but, *bam*, baby don't want a bar of it... *Give me that titty woman*. So, this is the hard part – you naturally kick in to mum mode and do what you can to survive, which is constantly feed the baby. Bub is trying to bring your milk in because those little drops of colostrum they had earlier just weren't enough... so they feed, feed, feed to increase your milk supply, and then all of a sudden, *hooray*, you have peace. Baby has finally got a little more milk to fill their marble-sized gut, then you and your boobs can get a well-deserved break for two to three hours... but don't be alarmed if this isn't the case for you and the cluster feeding commences again as they continue to try to bring your milk in. Also – please don't feel like a failure if you are unable to settle your baby... it is not a sign of *no* milk... some babies just need additional settling or top-ups.

Alfie *did not* settle on night two. I thought the first night was bad enough but night two was worse. Not even my titty could help him, so the midwife took charge, insisting I sleep for at least two hours while she whisked him away to spend the night at the desk with her. She swaddled him like a burrito, shoved his dummy in and, what do you know, he slept a solid three hours!!! Thank god, because I was starting to hallucinate and see rainbows and unicorns in my room

While we love our visitors, family and friends, indeed we need them, we also need time to be just us, a new family unit.

The (very) early days

due to two days of sleep deprivation. The struggle and juggle can be real, mumma, so please reach out to your midwife if you need help. I can't guarantee they'll be able to mind bub for you while you rest but they may be able to use some of their golden midwifery settling skills to pop your little one off to sleep. If you can, rest during day two before night falls, that way you will be a little more ready to face the night ahead. Also, now is a good time to give your baby any colostrum you may have expressed and stored antenatally. They will definitely appreciate a little top-up on this night. Just know it is normal for them to want to feed around the clock right now, for good reason. Trust your baby and trust your milk.

The dummy choice

I love the dummy. Like *really* love the dummy. There, I said it. And don't hate me for it. The dummy is called a pacifier for a reason and, guess what, it really can pacify your baby. Remember how I just spoke about night two and the cluster feeding? God damn this little rubber/silicone/plastic device can give your nips a good half-hour of reprieve, and despite what many think, no, it won't hinder your breastfeeding journey if you still feed your baby when they require a feed.

The Fourth Trimester

I remember one midwife saying to me, 'You should have your baby sucking your breast not that dummy.' I replied, 'Totally agree, however, my baby has sucked my boob for the last two hours and fifteen minutes and now I can't feel my nipples.' She gave me an awkward smirk and walked off. Like ffs – *sometimesssss* our nipples need a reprieve, just for half an hour at least! It is up to the parent to set the boundaries with the dummy, but I am a sucker and fell in love with it as much as my kids did because it legit provided them comfort when they needed it – even if it meant each of them, excluding Coco, had a dummy until they were three.

So, do you pack it in your hospital bag? I say go for it. Do you give it to baby straight after birth? Nope, not necessary. Just keep it for times when you are unable to settle your baby and they need some pacifying from something other than your boob.

I also personally believe dummies teach babies to suck better (unpopular opinion) . . . and if you have a colicky/reflux baby (I pray you don't), that a dummy will be more than a godsend. Babies suck to soothe, whether that be your breast or the dummy, you make the decision, just *pleaseeeeeee* don't mistake hunger for comfort.

Like anything, there are of course potential disadvantages in allowing your baby to use a dummy, such as the potential to cause misaligned teeth, confusing hunger signs for baby being just whingy, negative sleep association, affecting their communication or lack of. It is definitely up to you as the parent to do your research before making your decision, but knowing that it could potentially reduce the risk of SIDS (sudden infant death syndrome) made me feel a lot more comfortable with my decision to introduce the dummy. Just be sure not to attach the dummy to your baby's clothes or blankets with a cord or string due to the risk of injury or strangulation.

Alfie absolutely loved his dummy in hospital because of his sore head post-birth; he much preferred sucking the dummy than my breasts, despite my best efforts to try to constantly feed. Essie also loved hers. She was very complacent with boobie then a dummy plug to settle. Coco was never a dummy fan. She much preferred my breasts. So far so good with Scout – she doesn't really get a choice because being the fourth baby she has to be so patient.

Immunisations and tests for bub post-birth

This part of the postnatal period is often not discussed antenatally or is forgotten about until the time comes. Immunisations are not mandatory in Australia but are highly recommended by all paediatricians and doctors. Immunisations don't have to be overcomplicated, so I will give you a basic run-down.

Vitamin K

First up after birth we have the vitamin K injection – this one is not in fact an immunisation but a vitamin that is recommended in the few hours post-birth to help with blood clotting and to prevent bleeding. Babies are born with minimal vitamin K as they don't receive enough through pregnancy or breastfeeding. Without adequate vitamin K in the baby's body they can develop a rare disorder called vitamin K deficiency bleeding, which can ultimately lead to death. It is super rare but it can happen, hence the recommendation for the vitamin K injection. Personally, I gave these to all my babies without a second thought, but of course do your research. Myself, I recommend.

Hepatitis B

Next up we have the hepatitis B injection. This immunisation speaks for itself. Bub has their first dose within the first few days post-birth (ideally before leaving the hospital) and will have further doses given up until age four. The reason behind the push to give the hep B vaccine at birth is because many women (mothers) carry the disease without knowing it, and it can easily

The (very) early days

be transmitted to your baby. If you are known to carry hep B, your bub will be given hep B immunoglobulin post-birth for added protection.

Newborn screen test

Forty-eight to seventy-two hours post-birth your baby will be offered the NST (newborn screen test), which is a simple heel-prick test to collect a few blood droplets to test for rare diseases that, when left untreated, can have dire consequences on bub. To me, this test is a no-brainer – it isn't an immunisation, it isn't injecting anything into baby, it is simply a basic blood test which tests for super serious diseases. I feel we are blessed to be offered this and find out quite quickly post-birth if anything is wrong with our dear little bubs. I must say that over my ten-year career I have only had one patient decline, because they felt their baby would have long-term trauma from a minute needle prick. Each to their own. And honestly, most babies comfortably sit through this super quick test as we often perform it while they are feeding or sleeping deeply. The biggest annoyance for them is us holding their foot still, *ha*! If only babies could talk, I am sure that's what they would say.

Newborn hearing screen

The least invasive test of all is the newborn hearing screen. It is a simple hearing test that has your baby looking like a DJ while sound asleep in their hospital bassinet. A small number of babies are born with hearing loss which, if left untreated, could result in them developing a delay in speech and language skills. Although this test is not 100 per cent conclusive it does give you an indication if there is a hearing deficit post-birth. You will be told as soon as bub has concluded the test whether they have passed or failed. If they have failed, a follow-up test will be recommended in the coming weeks.

Jaundice testing

One other test your baby might be recommended to have post-birth is a screening test for jaundice (non-invasive), or an SBR (serum bilirubin level) blood test, which is more accurate, to check their jaundice levels. Jaundice is a very common occurrence in babies and often resolves with no treatment, but on occasion phototherapy (blue light therapy) may be recommended to help bub break down and excrete their jaundice levels more quickly. Your midwife and or paediatrician will keep an eye on your baby if they think bub is jaundiced. If they are, it is another reason to feed, feed, feed as babe being well hydrated can help to flush out the jaundice.

My babies were all a little jaundiced but didn't require any intervention. I also immunised all my

―――――

Your baby just wants mum.
Your baby needs good feeds.
You, the mother, need to rest
and restore. Your partner also
needs downtime and TLC.

―――――

children as soon as they were born, and continue to get the recommended vaccine schedule. This immunisation thing is a personal choice though. Not my circus, not my monkey, but as a health professional, and after reading copious amounts of research and working within my scope of practice, I must say I am very pro-vaccination. Each to their own, I say.

The baby blues

The good old baby blues that have you looking into a dark hole, weeping the day away with no answer as to why you are so emotional and why everything feels so irrational and overwhelming. Hold on mumma, it will settle. It won't be this way forever – generally the baby blues shouldn't last more than a few days and shouldn't be debilitating. If it is horrific and the black hole seems endless, see your GP as soon as you can. Be open with your health nurse and your partner. Share your thoughts and feelings with anyone who will listen because I can guarantee you aren't the first and certainly won't be the last to ever feel this way.

Women affected by the baby blues generally find it coincides with their milk coming in (around day three to five), but I get hit with the baby blues later then the norm. It always grabs me by the throat around

The (very) early days

day ten. It targets me after a long first week at home – following a lovely blues-free stay in hospital – when my exhaustion is next level, my adrenaline has well and truly dissipated, my energy stores are non-existent and the reality of three-hourly night wakings are in full force. It only lasts twenty-four hours for me but, man, I feel rough as hell, and doom and gloom holds my hands until I get through to the other side. On this note, your partner won't understand it completely either, but they will absolutely be feeling the pinch of your distress. The best thing they can do for you is make you endless cuppas, give you lots of cuddles, let you snooze, tell you it will be okay and give you unlimited support while you get through this. And you will. The most important thing for you to know is that you aren't alone – up to 80 per cent of women experience the baby blues and for most they seem to be short-lived. But you know yourself better than anyone, so if it doesn't feel right, it probably isn't.

I have been lucky to escape postnatal depression with my four kids; however, nine months postpartum after baby number two, Essie, postnatal anxiety knocked me for six out of nowhere. Seeing my GP immediately and having the support of Ambrose and my family and friends made the world of difference. I really believe to enjoy motherhood you need to have sound mental health and support.

Differentiating between the baby blues and depression or anxiety, or any postnatal mental health issue for that matter, is super-dooper important. And the same goes for your partner, as they too can be affected. It's important to remember that the baby blues shouldn't exceed a few days of feeling just that – 'blue'. Mood swings, overwhelm, bouts of anxiety, teariness, feeling flat should all disappear within a few days. If they don't or if you aren't coping full stop with your suspected baby blues, I can't stress enough the importance of checking in with your GP or care provider. Motherhood shouldn't be making you feel anxious, depressed, lousy, out of sorts or not like yourself for days on end in the early days. The changes we experience as women are unbelievable, and given no one actually knows exactly why we get the baby blues (though we assume hormones play a big part), it is always better to play it safe and see your doctor. So many other mummas and partners are in the same boat as you, and your doctor should welcome you with open arms if you're feeling this way. The best-case scenario is that you get the reassurance and treatment you need. In motherhood, nothing is off limits and I think it's important to acknowledge that. Motherhood changes you in more ways than one, and your baby needs you and your mental health to be in the best place possible. Lastly, be kind

The (very) early days

to yourself. Gosh, if I could wrap you in my arms and tell you it will all be okay (which it will at some stage, I promise), I would. Instead, I really hope you can feel my love and warmth through the pages of this book while you read my (hopefully) postnatal words of wisdom.

CHAPTER 6

Home time – the first week

Leaving hospital

You best believe you are about to embark on a bigger journey than bringing your baby into the world. Heading home for the very first time with your baby is so damn exciting, but also really ridiculously, terrifyingly anxiety provoking. The hospital room pack-up is a nervous one. *What the bloody hell have I forgotten? I swear I had an extra two swaddles. Where are my breast pads? Did you get the phone charger out of the wall? Should we take the pretty, dying, smelly flowers home?*

The Fourth Trimester

Best not in case baby has an allergy, right? Even better, let's hand them to the midwife station where they might get an extra day out of them. Then comes the whole *Shit, will we make it home in time before bub's next feed?* My best advice: just go. Your baby will survive the car drive home, as will you. Hint, hint: dummy is really handy here, *ha*! Speaking of the car ride home, don't even bother sitting in the front seat, we all know your heart will be far more relaxed squashed right there next to bub in the capsule. Before you take off, you feel like your pad is leaking. No doubt about it. You reposition it to hopefully catch the dribbles of blood seeping out, all before yelling at your partner to hurry up and get out of the car park. Did you know every partner drives 20 kilometres slower on the way home from hospital with their baby? It's true. They sit really close to the windscreen, they turn the music down to focus, they acclimatise the car heater appropriately and they clutch the wheel as tight as when they hold their baby. They take an extra five seconds at every corner, they give way to every Tom, Dick and Harry ... you just want to get bloody home.

 You turn into your street, and you breathe the biggest sigh of relief. Hallelujah, the baby and the boobs survived their very first car trip, but now you need to make it inside. You clasp the capsule and lift, but it won't move. *What the fuck have I done here?*

―――――――

The intro to your fourth
trimester was so brief in
the hospital, the real fun
begins here in your home . . .
rest assured, there are lots
of sunshine and rainbows
to come.

―――――――

you think to yourself. Great, another setback. *Will I ever make it inside?* A few jiggles and *bam* the capsule dislodges, and your baby momentarily opens their eyes to only shut them again seconds later. Home. *We are home.* You breathe. The dog barks to welcome you all and you shuffle gently inside while your partner moves behind you, capsule in hand, at snail's pace. And so it begins. Your new life at home. The intro to your fourth trimester was so brief in the hospital, the real fun begins here in your home, with your new baby, your depressed cat and whimpering dog and delicate partner. But rest assured, there are lots of sunshine and rainbows to come. In fact, you might be on cloud nine right now and your dog might be doing laps of excitement with you. But together, let's navigate what lies ahead in the next few months.

Baby products: So many choices

Let's start with the relentless baby products. If there is one thing I am definitely an expert with after four kids it's the baby product must-haves. It is easy to get upsold these days, especially with social media throwing every baby product in our face, but what I know for certain is you do not need an expensive pram. Let's start with that. Their prices range from $350 to $3500 and that

Home time – the first week

is just insanity. They all do the same thing. What you want is one that can completely recline and doesn't weigh 30 kilos. In saying that, is the bassinet attachment necessary? Not really, as babies spend such a short amount of time in it, but if you really want it, then go for it. A pram that reclines back the entire way is perfect and, dare I say, far less bulky. These prams also fold up in one go, which is brilliant. I have trialled every damn pram there is and those that take up the whole boot are beyond draining. Compact is key.

Next: the bassinet. This is a temporary item remember. Babies only stay in them for as long as they can fit, then they move into a cot. While I do love a bassinet, once again, you don't need a super expensive one. They all do the same thing. And let's be real, they pretty much just stay in the same spot for the next few months in your room anyway. I get the hype though; especially for our first babies, we want the best of the best.

The capsule: *yes*, everyone needs one of these. I am a big, big fan, and the best part? You don't have to buy one, you can rent them dirt cheap for a six-month period. Win, win!

The nappy bag is another money stealer. You don't need one with an expensive label attached. I started off with a $300 nappy bag (a baby shower gift from the girls) and, while it was cute, I ended up using a cheap-ass bag from Kmart that I could throw in the wash every now and then. By baby number four you end up just shoving a nappy and wipes under your pram. Well, I do anyway.

One thing that is a must-have is a baby bouncer – one that baby can safely sit in when your arms need a break. I used to plonk mine on my kitchen bench while I prepared dinner and worked through witching hour. They don't have to be expensive, just safe and practical.

The first week at home

Shall we start at the first week at home? Generally, you will have either just spent five or so days in a private hospital post-birth, or three days, if you are fortunate enough, in the public system. Three days is generally for those patients who have had a caesarean section. Three days is generous for our public health system. By this stage you will have taken up your position on the couch at home, feet up, cuppa in hand and fielding a million calls and texts from family and friends eager to pop in and meet baby. But what about you? What about mumma?

Many women are coming home to their other children, where the chaos continues, and life quickly

Home time – the first week

returns to normal. But for those women experiencing new motherhood, this is their first time bringing new life into the world and all of a sudden they are supposed to have their shit together, feed and protect the baby, while having a world of visitors flood their house, smothering their new baby in cuddles and kisses and smears of lipstick, and at the same time, sitting there answering birth questions and smiling awkwardly when all they want to do is lay their ass down on that couch and cut everyone's arms off so they don't stir the baby. It's a lot and it's just the start.

The first week home doesn't only see you navigating your visitors, you are also navigating your life as a new mum. The sun still rises every day, yet it now hits differently. The two- to three-hourly overnight wakings slowly become your new norm and the rising sun is a reminder of the new day that lies ahead, leaving behind the minimal sleep you got the day before. Here we are again. Groundhog day of your new life together.

You feed, change the nappy, feed again, clear the messy bedside from the night that was, attempt to put baby down while you grab a one-minute shower, but that's all too hard, you will wait for hubby to get back from fetching you a fresh coffee from the local coffee shop that *he* got to walk too by *himself*, all alone while you nourish your little one. Yes, you heard that right, you can have caffeine even if you are a breastfeeding mumma. In terms of actual caffeine intake, our babies take in approximately 1 per cent of our caffeine intake, and it peaks in breastmilk an hour after consumption. I will leave it up to your discretion, but be mindful, if your baby seems unsettled or jittery, it could be that caffeine affecting them.

I am not one to glorify things, if you haven't noticed yet – I call a spade a spade. Sure, there are women who sprint out of bed with perfectly managed breasts and somehow cook up a three-course brekkie for their hardworking partner and four kids before they get off to school, but these mummas, I tell you, are the minority. I wish I was like them. I would love to have my shit together. To not feel like I have broken-back syndrome 24/7 and have my head spinning in circles. I would also love to shower for twenty minutes in peace and apply my make-up and tan and squeeze into my tiny pre-baby leggings, but the reality for me is that my gut is still so swollen and saggy, my boobs are too sore to wear a maternity crop and my eyes are so fucking heavy that if I can squeeze thirty-eight ninety-second micro naps in before I have to start my day, I will.

For the love of god, stay off Instagram. You will be bombarded with five-star morning routines and 'How I got my body back after the baby' videos. Then you will start receiving ads left, right and centre promoting the

Home time – the first week

world's best weight-loss supp and at-home workout subscriptions. You know, the kind that makes you want to vomit but tempts you at the same time. It's a rabbit hole . . . a deep, dark rabbit hole.

So, the first week at home will be broken sleep, poo-stained blankets, vomit-filled burp cloths, nervous baby bath times, tears, joy, laughter, smiles and tight cuddles from your partner. There will be head shakes and *what the actual fuck* moments. Your Google browser will stay open and Uber Eats will be stalking you to place yet another meal order. You will have your first appointment with your designated Maternal and Child Health nurse and you may manage a walk around the block. No pressure though, it's about getting some fresh air and vitamin D, not getting your body back. Baby snugs will be high on your priority list and no doubt you will snooze together at any interval you can. Most partners are on leave with you for the first few weeks, so for the first week at least they will be your snack bitch, chef, hydrator, psychologist, cheerleader, nappy changer, food shopper, visitor sergeant, washing hanger, floor cleaner, dog walker and voice of reason. Well, hopefully.

I remember my first week at home with Alfie. I felt good. Too good – I was going to be walking up shit hill soon. I made an effort to do my make-up every day and I felt amazing for doing so. I cooked and cleaned

Sure, there are women who . . . cook up a three-course brekkie for their hardworking partner and four kids before they get off to school, but these mummas, I tell you, are the minority.

Home time – the first week

and drank way too many cups of tea with my never-ending visitors and struggled to switch off to sleep come night-time. I went for a few gentle walks, did a food shop on my own and spent 99 per cent of my time awake, feeding my chubby baby, which included, no bullshit, every two hours overnight. Safe to say this happy hormone bubble I was 'thriving' in soon popped and then my reality check of the fourth trimester came to fruition. I knew it was too good to be true. My big energy levels quickly depleted, and I entered sleep school six months postpartum. I could write a whole book on sleep alone. Instead, I will touch on the basics of baby sleep in Chapter 9.

Let's not also forget this first week at home is a time to recover, recover, recover from your vaginal or caesarean birth. Particularly post-caesarean you really need to avoid any heavy lifting (including your washing and the toddler) and spend your days resting, with some gentle walking and elevation of your legs while reclining thrown into the mix. Of course, post-vaginal the same may apply, especially if you have had an instrumental (forceps/vacuum) birth. Actually, screw all of that – no one lift anything heavy or do any household chores, your pelvic floor will thank you for it.

The Maternal and Child Health nurse

I want to introduce you to your Maternal and Child Health nurse. Someone who will be with you for the first four years of your bub's life. They sometimes receive a bad rap from the social media community or even from someone you know for the advice they impart or the way they impart it. They may indeed be abrupt at times – heck, anyone in this profession can be – but in fact they are a wealth of knowledge. Trust me, they know their shit. Sometimes, yes, they should wrap you in a cuddle instead of making jerky remarks *but* they truly do have your best interests at heart. Their role is to help you and your baby to thrive and to be content. Yes, they want your baby to gain weight. They also will be your close mental health advocate.

Your health nurse will check important things like the colour of your baby to determine if any jaundice is present. They will also look at your baby's umbilical button to make sure it isn't infected and is being managed appropriately. It may have fallen off by now, which is even better. They will check baby's reflexes too. They will suggest ways to play with your baby and discuss your sleeping arrangements to ensure baby is sleeping safely. They will be taking note of your emotional well-being and assist with any breast or

Home time – the first week

bottle feeds you need help with. Really, they will be watching you more closely than you are aware of, but all for good cause. They want you to feel physically, mentally and emotionally supported with a thriving baby.

I was blessed with wonderful health nurses for my four kids – all easy to talk to and intuitive enough to wrap the appointments up as quickly as possible, as I always had another child with me itching to get out of there. They weighed and measured my baby, and asked all of the important questions: if I felt mentally okay, if I needed any feeding assistance, if I had recovered from birth. You know, all the things you wish they could be there for at 2 am.

I advise you to go into your appointments with an open mind and heart, and ignore any negative comments you may have heard from your friends. If the nurse asks you how you are feeling, be honest. They aren't going to slap a postnatal depression sticker on your head, they will simply reassure you about what is normal and what's not. You may be lucky enough to have your very first visit in your own lounge room where they will observe you feeding and then gently strip bub off and put them on the scales. I know how you will be feeling right at that moment: your eyes will be piercing holes into the numbers on the scale as they stabilise and confirm a weight, hopefully a high one. And you will either breathe a sigh of relief at the results or cringe deep inside, asking what more you can do for your baby in order to see those numbers climb a little higher.

If your baby hasn't reached the desired weight, firstly, be aware that scales are never 100 per cent accurate. Secondly, your baby is a week old – don't be hard on yourself or them. Thirdly, if you are breastfeeding there is a big chance your milk is only fully coming in now. Lastly, everything that seems problematic can be solved. It is the weight losses, not the slow gains, that can cause soft alarm bells to ring for the health nurse. But remember, their job is to make sure you are both well and baby is growing according to the appropriate centile chart.

Sometimes you can't win either way, though, I will be honest. If your baby hasn't gained anything you might want to cut your boobs off and shove a bottle down their throat, *or*, on the flip side, your baby has gained way more than the 'average norm' and you are told to slow the feeds down and space them out. Just use this first appointment as a starting point in your feeding journey and plan from there. *Everything is fixable*, I promise. My best advice is to take on the nurse's feedback, pick what will work for you and stick to it. By the next visit I am sure any feeding issues that may have been highlighted will be resolving and you will feel like you are getting a hold of this whole mum gig.

If you are lucky enough to have a wonderful health nurse like I did, you will fall in love with them and look forward to the next catch up and weigh-in.

Common health challenges for your baby

Colic versus reflux

Chances are you will have heard of colic and reflux, but if you haven't, they would have to be among the most googled topics in the first few months of having a baby. First and foremost, your baby will cry. This is normal. This is how they communicate. But to what degree? Determining the difference between your baby just crying because they are hungry or tired as opposed to crying because they are in pain with colic or reflux is a challenging thing. Learning the difference between colic and reflux is helpful, but to know for sure, a visit to the doctor is needed to diagnose and confirm.

Colic is essentially long periods of crying for no apparent reason accompanied by the baby being extremely hard to settle. It peaks around week two and can last until four months of age. The crying is often worse in the evening, which is I guess why a lot of people refer to this time as the witching hour. Colic does not have a medical explanation but you should always see your GP if you're concerned with your baby's crying to exclude anything more sinister. I survived this period with plenty of baby wearing, arvo walks with bub in the pram and a *lot* of breastfeeding while binge-watching TV.

Reflux is a little different. It occurs when the contents of a baby's stomach travels back up the oesophagus. Generally, babies suffering from reflux will either vomit frequently with or without distress, or swallow the contents instead of expelling them (also known as silent reflux). These babies tend to still thrive but have disrupted sleep, gastric upset and present as unsettled. This is a very common reason parents visit the GP in the early days, and be aware that if the GP diagnoses reflux or GORD (gastro-oesophageal reflux disease – a more severe case of reflux), they may gently medicate to reduce symptoms. Rest assured, not every baby will require medication and most outgrow it by the age of one; however, this definitely needs a medical diagnosis.

Intolerances and allergies

I am not qualified to diagnose medical conditions, intolerances or allergies; however, as an IBCLC it is usually easy to spot a baby that has a suspected lactose or cow's milk protein intolerance or allergy because

---

So, the first week at home
will be broken sleep, poo-
stained blankets, vomit-filled
burp cloths, nervous baby
bath times, tears, joy, laughter,
smiles and tight cuddles from
your partner.

---

they present with similar symptoms. They always need to be reviewed by a doctor for diagnosis.

My baby Scout was diagnosed by her paediatrician at two weeks of age with CMPI (cow's milk protein intolerance) after an extreme all-over body rash kept getting more aggressive. She was *very* unsettled, had intense stomach pains, explosive poo and, even worse, blood in her stool (poo). Note to yourself: if your baby has any of these symptoms it's always worth a check-up as soon as possible, especially if there is blood in their stools. There is no formal way to diagnose this, apart from assessing symptoms. After eliminating all dairy and soy from my diet, within a few days I had a completely content baby. Her rash disappeared in forty-eight hours, her gas and tummy upset settled immensely, her fussiness was gone and there was no longer any blood in her poo. Looking back, I swear Coco and Alfie had this too, although it wasn't commonly diagnosed then.

The good news is most babies will outgrow CMPI as they enter their toddler/preschool years.

Hint, hint: see your doctor and always advocate for your child if it doesn't feel right for you or them.

Purple crying
This one is rarely spoken about. But it is a real thing. Purple crying is described as a period for new babies

when they are crying more than normal and can't be settled or soothed. According to the Sydney Children's Hospital Network, the 'purple' stands for:

- **Peak** – is usually between six to eight weeks of age, and tends to settle down around the third or fourth month.
- **Unexpected** – the crying seems to come out of nowhere.
- **Resists soothing** – the baby can no longer be settled, and they might continue to cry even when new strategies are tried.
- **Pain** – the baby might look like they are in pain or are gassy, and can't get relief.
- **Long-lasting** – the baby might cry for hours at a time.
- **Evening** – these periods of crying are more common in the evening but can happen at any time of the day.

I swear this happens to a lot of babies, but of course not all. I think my babies each suffered from purple crying at least once. Naturally I freaked and paid a visit to the GP to ensure there was nothing more sinister going on. There wasn't. Here is hoping you and your babe will bypass this, but as with all these issues, don't be afraid to seek help from your GP for any health concerns or worries.

Your first week feeding on your own

Congrats! You have managed to nourish your baby in hospital and now it's time to do it on your own at home without buzzing a midwife for assistance. I am going to start by telling you this: you can do it! In the beginning it will be hard, not just for you, but for your baby too. Sure, breastfeeding is 'natural' but the only thing really natural about it is that the milk is produced in your very own body. It is actually a skill. A learned skill for both you and your baby. And if I am honest, it will take a good six weeks until you can latch baby without three pillows and a sting. I truthfully think the hardest part of the first week at home is confidently attaching baby to the breast. The key is not to overcomplicate it. Your baby is hungry so you feed. Your baby is weeing and pooing regularly so your baby is getting your milk. Your baby is gaining appropriate amounts of weight so they are getting enough milk. Your breasts are feeling softer after a feed, therefore your baby is draining your milk.

How do we make breastfeeding at home as easy as possible for mum and bub? You don't need a super fancy chair, or a $250 breastfeeding pillow. You just need a comfy spot with good back support and an environment where you can comfortably flop your titties out while you try to latch this gorgeous thing.

Home time – the first week

You need an infinite amount of time and zero pressure, even from yourself.

First things first, if your baby is screaming at you, they will not feed. How on earth are you going to jam a breast into the mouth of an irritated baby desperate for a feed but giving no cooperation by constantly arching the back, kicking the legs and bellowing cries? Calm baby first. Pat, cuddle, swaddle, dummy, clean finger suck . . . do what you can to try to calm them, then start again. Okay, deep breath – you have got this mumma! See, that is better . . . once baby is calm, place them in a cradle or football hold, put your big nipple to their nose and when they open their little itty-bitty mouth you place as much nipple and breast in the mouth as possible. Naturally, your baby should automatically start sucking. If it doesn't feel right, like the ouch is super ouchy, remove baby and start again. It should feel better the next time. Sounds so easy right? But I know it's not. Generally, while we are trying to latch baby on we have dripping nips soaking our tops, smelly underarms making us gag when we get a whiff of them, a racing heart and a super tight clenched body and neck that *reallllly* needs to relax once baby is on. Remember – if you are anxious, baby feels every inch of it and struggles to settle. Your cortisol spikes theirs. So chill mumma, big deep breaths.

Babies have no filter. They can be really rude

actually. One minute they are subtly licking their lips and forty-five seconds later screaming at you to feed them. A clever idea for you from a mum, midwife and sleep consultant is to get baby on before they get to the screaming stage. Wake them gently by unswaddling them just before their feed is due or if it has reached the three-hour mark since their last feed. Take their hands out of their mittens and let them have a big stretch on your lap while your big boobs are staring at them in the face with little droplets of milk dripping on their nose. When you are ready, gently guide them onto the breast as I described above. It should be easier to attach them this way than when they are a screaming banshee desperate for a suckle. And guess what, if you fail miserably and they just want to sleep instead, strip them nudie rudie and change their nappy to wake them. That should do the trick.

Think of it like this, especially when you are beyond exhausted: the better and longer you make each feed, the more settled your baby will be in between feeds and the greater your chance of having some time to switch off. A well-fed baby is a content one and I stand by this.

No doubt about it – our babies must thrive to survive, right? So it's no wonder we become hyper-focused on feeding. The thing that complicates many new mums' feeding journey is all the advice from Judie,

Home time – the first week

Trudie and Susie. *Keep him on longer. He is feeding too long. She has fallen asleep, let me hold her. He needs a bottle. Just give him a bottle. She looks unsettled – want me to feed her for you?* Can everyone politely shut up?! You are the mother, you know what is best for your baby, back yourself in and back everyone off. And a note to anyone reading this who has previously had kids: *pleaseeeeeee* keep your opinions to yourself unless they are asked for. It does nothing but confuse a new mum, destroy their confidence and fill us with self doubt. The best thing *you* can do for this mumma is make her a cuppa and make your visit brief. And I mean that in the nicest possible way. New mummas are already so self-critical that any miniscule piece of unwanted advice or judgement can be super detrimental and feel soul-shattering.

The next question I am sure you are wondering about is *How do I know if I have given a long enough feed?* There are no set rules in breastfeeding. You'll hear all sorts of suggestions and recommendations: fifteen minutes each side; thirty minutes one side only; a sixty-minute feed; or just feed until baby is content. The reality is the moment your baby starts sucking, the milk supply increases and they often appear 'done' and 'asleep' after five minutes. Great right? Not really, because after just a five-minute feed, bub will be screaming an hour later for another.

Babies have no filter. They can be really rude actually. One minute they are subtly licking their lips and forty-five seconds later screaming at you to feed them.

Home time – the first week

I say trust yourself – you will soon know what makes your baby content and how much is enough for your little babe. I always aim for a good twenty-minute feed on one breast – unless they are actively sucking well longer than this – then a nappy change, a quick stretch and a top-up from the other side. Some babies take both sides well, others zip their mouths up for the second breast as they are full to the brim. So, it's simple: offer the feed on the other side, if they won't take it, fine, start on that breast at the next feed. If that breast is *bursting* at the seams and super uncomfy then, sure, express a *little* bit to make it comfortable but be careful not to increase the supply too much or you will end up on the mastitis merry-go-round. If you are not familiar with mastitis, it is when your breast/s becomes inflamed because of nipple damage (bacteria can enter there into the breast causing infection) or a change to your milk ducts. Another common cause of mastitis is the inability to drain breastmilk adequately, causing inflammation and/or blocked ducts.

To best judge that your baby is feeding well, observe them. Follow their lead. If they are passed out dead to the world, snoozing away after a good suckle, have a full nappy at the next feed, and last at least three hours between feeds, well done, your supply is adequate and baby is content. If you have a baby that won't settle, is irritable and trying to latch to anything in sight, won't settle or sleep, then baby needs a bigger, longer feed.

If you are feeling unsure, you can always hire a lactation consultant who can help in all aspects of breastfeeding, as I mentioned in Chapter 4. Overall, you are doing a bloody good job mumma. No one tells you how draining this part of raising a baby is.

Visitors at home

This is for visitors. We love you. We need you. We appreciate you. But don't ruin it. Don't overdo it. Don't overstay. Don't take offence when we space out mid convo. If we are spending more in other parts of the house than engaging in conversation on the couch with you, take a hint. I feel like there should be a standard rule that no one can stay for longer than forty-five minutes. Another rule for visitors should be that you can't enter unless you come bearing gifts of the good kind. A fresh coffee for mum. A Baker's Delight bun. If I don't see a dish with foil over the top, turn around and go home. *Haha.* Could you imagine? But you get my drift. Visit, sure, but come with the good stuff and leave before we need to feed the baby again.

Also – I am just putting it out there – I think most

Home time – the first week

people would find it awkward if you ask to fold our washing. I mean, if you aren't grandma, then it feels kinda strange. I don't think your friend Sally from accounts really wants to fold your blood-stained granny jocks anyway, despite feeling obligated to offer. Thanks anyway but no thanks.

One last thing, visitors – don't offer to 'watch' or 'hold' the baby while we have a nap. We just can't do that. We would rather have our dog watch over the baby than have you sit staring at the wall in our lounge room while we try to doze off into slumber land in our bedroom away from our baby. That whole *Have a lie down and I will watch bub for you* has good merit and the right intentions but is quite impossible to achieve. Am I wrong?

A few other things visitors should be made aware of: avoid rank perfume. I get it, you want to smell nice. Appreciate that. We won't stop you from wearing it, but we just ask that you don't douse yourself in a litre of it. Certainly, don't bother wearing Red Door by Elizabeth Arden. We would rather vomit. If you smoke, make sure you scrub those hands if you insist on touching the baby. If you are sick, just cancel. Even a sniffle isn't cool. Don't kiss my baby. Just don't make it awkward for us. If my baby cries, please hand it back to me. Baby just wants its mumma. Lastly, don't post my baby on social media unless I say so. I will let you know if it's okay to expose bub to potential internet creeps, but for now more biscuits and cakes please.

When your partner returns to work

The moment you either dread or have been *hanginggg* for: the day your partner heads back to work. I bet you had a restless sleep the night before. For most, it is entirely anxiety-provoking knowing you have to cross this next bridge by yourself. Just when you slowly started to find your rhythm at home together as a family, now you must re-route your days without your partner and somehow survive the swell that lies ahead.

What we don't often think about, or tend to forget, is how *they* are feeling leaving us behind. Do they want to go back to work? Will they miss us? Will they cope? If your name is Ambrose you will probably jump at the prospect of uninterrupted work and coffee time without kids. It can mean long lunches, adult conversations, zero nappies, bugger all chores. This is when you may feel a pang of resentment or jealousy about the freedom they have compared to you. I mean, sure, you can go back to work now too, but you do realise what you are doing is the most important work of all, don't you? The hardest of jobs. The most challenging

Home time – the first week

promotion. The most costly yet satisfying job around. Don't wish your time away mumma, the day will come sooner then you anticipate to part with bub.

So how on earth do we in fact do this parenting on our own while our partner goes back to work? It is a whole new learning experience. One that you will navigate with your mothers' group or mumma friends. One where you will end up finding your own little routine and ways to go about your day. One that will see you excited to binge on your fave TV show while the baby naps. One that will leave you feeling so empowered, you can take on the world. Do you know how hard it is to keep another human fed, happy, clean and healthy? It's hard but you can do it. And you will do it. And some days you will love the autonomy and other days you will want to email your boss and tell them you want to start back first thing Monday. I told you motherhood is wild.

The day your partner returns to work is when you will need to begin prioritising some 'me' time. You will need to schedule in at least thirty minutes a day to yourself or you legit will go batshit crazy. It's good for you, good for your baby and good for your partner. Whether it is a long shower, a walk, a gym sesh, food shopping, clothes shopping, mindless scrolling, a nap, a coffee with a friend, a blow wave or an extended shit in peace, you deserve it and need it. That cup depletes

The Fourth Trimester

super quick I hate to tell you. It is your job, with the help of others, to keep it over halfway full.

If you are wondering what you will do with your time all day, well don't. You'll blink and it will be 4.30 pm and *The Bold and the Beautiful* will be blaring in the background. It will almost be bath and dinner time and you'll still be in your PJs from the night before. Cool, cool, cool. That's the beauty of being the stay-at-home mum. You can go at your own pace. It may see you unshowered for the day but, hey, who cares. This time is only temporary. One day when you are stuck in the traffic on your way to work, you will reminisce on these days and beg for them back.

Your days at home will go something like this when your partner returns to work: lazy sleep-in with baby after a rough night of feeding ... then you will clear the dirty nappies from the bedside table. You will pour a cup of coffee while you creep out on said sleeping baby. You will plan a trip to the shops to get some new clothes for yourself and some goodies for bub, except you probably won't make it due to said baby and feeling a tad overwhelmed. You will promise yourself tomorrow will be a new day, and it will be. Each morning you will wake up more confident than the day before, and your new normal will become more manageable. You will enjoy your day with bub no matter how exhausting it is, but there is no doubt

Home time – the first week

you will count down the time until your partner walks through the door to take the reins. Enjoy the challenges that each day may present as they will make you a stronger person, more resilient than ever. If you can manage to make it through the day with your little one, then you mumma are a superstar.

The first solo outing with bub

Whether you wait until bub has had their second round of vaccinations around six weeks or you hit the ground waddling days post-birth, an outing is just as important as your two and a half litres of water a day. Before you know it, you will be climbing the four walls of your asylum, desperate to catch some germs at your local shopping centre. Some crave the first outing and others tackle it head-on with dread. Far out it can be daunting. Throw a colic/reflux baby in there and oh my god it feels like you need to press a thousand panic buttons in one go.

My best advice: do some teeny-tiny practice runs first. Start with a basic, gentle walk around the block with bub in the pram. If you can master that ten-minute trip solo, you can absolutely tackle an outing to the shops or a friend's place. Slow and steady wins the race. And guess what? If it all gets too much,

Prior to venturing out on your own for the first time, do not overpack.

Home time – the first week

you just turn around and head back home. A crying baby doesn't last forever, nor does a car trip . . . if you feel too overwhelmed you will be back in your safe zone in no time. The more you practise the better you become at it.

Prior to venturing out on your own for the first time, do *not* overpack. How many mums do you see lugging around a mammoth backpack full of garbage? You don't need a whole tin of formula, sixteen bottles, eight swaddles, three hats, five hundred nappies, eight packets of baby wipes, five spew rags, ninety-two changes of baby clothes, your kitchen sink, your king-size bed and your oven. All you need (trust me when I say this) is a small pack of baby wipes, two nappies, one blanket, a dummy, one bottle made up ready to go, your set of titties if breastfeeding, your phone, keys and your sanity. That is all.

Let's be honest, the first outing you will last thirty-five minutes max before heading home again. My outings consist of a dummy shoved in my bra, leaking boobs, a twisted breast pad, a spewed-on swaddle and a water bottle and snack for myself, so I don't pass out from my anxiety trying to choke me to death. I'm not even joking. Slow, steady steps are key to gaining your confidence and independence.

CHAPTER 7

The days are long but the years are short – the first month

Whether it is your first time doing the fourth trimester . . .

First of all – I am super jealous. I would *love* to do the fourth trimester for the first time all over again, even with the horrific two-hourly night wakes for six months (no, this isn't normal). There is something so precious about the first time. The first everything with your first baby. You don't realise until you are doing it for the second or third or fourth time just how much you wish you'd soaked in more of the fourth trimester for the first time.

If you are reading this and about to have your first baby, then listen closely.

Do not move off the couch for the first few weeks. I have no idea why I never listened to everyone telling me to enjoy all the snuggles at home on the couch. Why did I feel the need to do everything all the time? Not sure if it was fear of missing out or anxiety, but I was way too busy for a first-time mum and I regret it. I mean, sure, at the time it was fun ... but looking back now I just burned myself out and never took enough time to mentally, physically and emotionally recharge in the fourth trimester.

If you are reading this with a baby in your arms, stay put. Don't let the world in, it's a trap. Once you share yourself and your baby there is no coming back. In many other countries new mums don't leave their bed for the first few weeks following the birth of their child. They believe that rest, warmth and good nutrition is key to healing emotionally, physically and mentally. Far out I wish we in Western culture followed suit. We put our bodies under so much pressure to bounce back following childbirth, it's no wonder many of us find ourselves staring down the barrel of postnatal anxiety and/or depression. If we took more time to ourselves

The first month

to rest and restore, all mothers would be far better off.

In saying this, and having experienced childbirth four times now, I have a list of key take-home messages to share with first-time parents.

Limit your visitors. I know you can't wait to show off your baby but be mindful visitors drain your battery like you wouldn't believe. They will also overstimulate your baby by holding and passing them around so much. By no means am I telling you to avoid visitors altogether, but for your own sanity and the protection of your baby, limit them. Also, it is *vital* that you reiterate to your visitors that if anyone is slightly unwell they cancel and reschedule their visit. In times like today, we need to protect ourselves and our babies more than ever.

Walk every day. Do not underestimate the power of fresh air and vitamin D. Not only is it good for your body physically, it is so good for the soul. It has proven to reduce anxiety and depression, so even five minutes of pounding the pavement is better than nothing. This is the only exception to moving off the couch in the first few weeks.

Talk to your friends. It doesn't have to be a phone call. Checking in via text is enough if that's all you can muster. It's good to keep them posted with how you are all doing.

Hydrate. Hydrate a shit load. (I need to remember

Do not move off the couch for
the first few weeks.

The first month

to take my own advice.) Hydrating is always so important, but particularly in these first few weeks. Even if you aren't breastfeeding or pumping it's so important you replenish your body with adequate water. The compounding effects of dehydration can wreak havoc on you without you even realising.

Be honest. Be honest with yourself and everyone else. Your mental health is an absolute priority always, especially during this volatile period. Talk to anyone who will listen. If you aren't coping, say something. There are no heroes in trying to keep it all together. The best way to feel and get better is to make your feelings known and speak to your GP asap. Poor mental health is rife in motherhood and we can all understand why.

Go to bed early. I mean this one. Tuck yourself into bed when you put bub down 'for the night'. Often when they go to bed for the night we find ourselves wanting time to ourselves, which is fair enough, but also often ends in us falling asleep just before their next feed. It's never fun to be woken up soon after falling into a deep sleep.

Try to eat healthy. Sounds simple. Take it from me, someone who shoved that much sugar into their mouth postpartum in an effort to stay awake. It never ends well – you feel way worse feeding your body crap instead of things it is actually depleted of.

Take everyone's unsolicited advice with a grain of salt. Everyone is *very* good at leaving their opinion on your doorstep. Believe me it will be given even if you didn't ask for it. Some advice may be helpful (the grandmas really do often have the best burping tricks) and some will not. By not I mean your 'helpful' friend suggesting a not-so-friendly sleep routine way before it's necessary.

Only you and your partner know best. Trust your gut. Your mum intuition is real. Don't fault it.

Book a date with your partner. Sounds ridiculous so early on but your time together is so, so important, particularly in this period of vulnerability. Partners often get left behind. Their emotional, physical and mental well-being is also important and we often forget this, which is understandable, but touching base with each other, even if only briefly, is really important. If grandma or your sister offers to babysit, take them up on it. It doesn't have to mean hours away from bub. It could just mean a quick lunch together at your local café.

Don't rush to get your body back. Listen to it. Sure, you may feel ready to run a marathon. Lucky you if this is the case. But most still feel tender at this stage. If you don't physically feel it, believe me your insides do. There is a reason we are told to wait a good six weeks before resuming any physical exercise or heavy

The first month

lifting, whatever your mode of birth. Without seeing it, our uterus is working hard internally to heal, not to mention our pelvic floor and organs. Take this time to be reasonably lazy for once. It's for a good cause this time.

It's okay to say no. I mean that. I was shocking at saying that word. I should have said it more. Especially when I made the jump from one to two babies. I put myself under so much pressure to have all the visitors over, to attend all the events even though I was exhausted, to accept invitations when all I wanted to do was sleep. It is pretty empowering using that word, so now is your time to put you and your new family first while you leave the guilt behind.

Invest in a cleaner. For real. I know we are all on budgets but if you can factor this one in it makes the world of difference to your postnatal recovery. Another approach is getting your friends to put in together for a cleaner as a baby shower gift . . . even if it's only for a one-off clean, it feels damn good not to have to lift a finger. It's a little 'treat yourself' kind of thing. Dog shat on the floor? *Meh*, the cleaner will disinfect properly tomorrow. Carpet is looking filthy . . . who cares, the cleaner will get it in a few days. The bathroom needs a scrub? Leave it to the cleaner.

The Fourth Trimester

... Or you're an 'old hand' at the fourth trimester ...

Not your first time facing this trimester? Come here old friend. This time hits different. I won't lie ... In my experience entering it for the second, third, fourth time is more challenging than the first. Sure, we know what to expect, but doing it while keeping not just one, but maybe two, three, four kids alive as well can be bloody demanding and difficult. Leave all of your expectations at the door and surrender to what will be. The pandemonium is only short-lived, I promise you. This time, you may want to accept more help than last time. And don't feel guilty if you do. Take the help. Ask for the help. Don't do it alone. Call upon your village.

I was recently discussing with a friend what we *really* need and want postpartum as mothers from our friends, family and visitors, and we felt it was this: help with our other kids. Not the baby. Sure, have a quick cuddle when you come to meet him/her, but more importantly, don't 'hang' and overstay. Come and play with our other kid(s). Take them to the park. Take them outside for us. Do a drawing with them. Read them a book. Make *them* feel special. Our guilt is already choking us, so please do us that favour. Or, if you are the friend or family member that isn't really that into kids, do the right thing and bring a

The first month

meal. I can't reinforce enough how good it was to have seven lasagnes dropped off in our first month home. Another hot tip: a fruit platter is always welcome too. Or a cheesecake. You bet we love a good cheesy with our morning cuppa.

Managing multiple kids at home with a newborn

It's all well and good to return home post-birth with one little human, but when you have a toddler hanging off your hip and older kids hanging off your legs, it can be, *ahhh*, somewhat challenging. People always ask what was harder for me. Going from none to one baby, or one to two. And now I have *four*. I can be honest and say that going from one to two was absolutely, hands down the hardest transition for me of all. Perhaps it was the two under two that choked me out, or the fact that Ambrose worked six days a week, ten- to twelve-hour days and I was stranded in my tiny home mothering a twenty-month-old toddler with more energy than a Duracell battery and a baby that only liked to sleep in her own bassinet. Let's just say it was a very trying time for me. But we got through, and this is how.

When the kids would wake, I'd feed the baby then

make a plate of toast for Alfie, throw on his jumper, change his stinky, wee-filled nappy from the night before and dash out the door damn quick before I regretted my decision. I would strap them both in the pram (until Alfie would unbuckle his straps and make a run for it) and pound the pavement for fifteen minutes around the block so I felt like I was doing *something* for my toddler. If I got out of the house first thing my guilt about being a boring mum wasn't there and Alfie would manage to burn some much-needed energy before the baby went down for her nap undisturbed.

If Alfie burned some energy, it meant I could put a movie on for some downtime for both of us while Essie had her morning sleep. This is *so* basic but does wonders, not just for our other children but for us mothers too. We all know how isolating and suffocating it can feel being nap-trapped inside all day, so I made a point to do this most days and what a difference it made to my mental state and energy levels, not to mention my bones as they managed to suck in some much-needed vitamin D. If you have toddler at home, your biggest challenge is going to be getting the newborn to sleep without teeny little hands and big loud voices startling them. Luckily, in the first few months babies tend to sleep anywhere and can tolerate most noise. If not, and you are really struggling to settle

The first month

bub with your toddler around, make a fun basket for them! It is something you let them play with that they are not normally allowed. My favourite was having a cheap Kmart toy hidden in the cupboard, or arts and crafts they would love. It should keep them interested while you duck in and out to do some settling without little footsteps following you.

In terms of coping in general as a mother, if you have older kids, use their help. My older two never shy away from assisting with bath time, pram pushes, nappy changes, dummy plugs, car songs, baby holds and outfit selections. This is the benefit of having a slightly bigger age gap this time around too. And, of course, don't forget to call upon your village for help when you need it. Your family, your friends, your neighbours, your GP, your partner. And if you have no one, message me. I will be there for you. Most of all, remember that this time really does go so fast.

Broken sleep

There is absolutely nothing in this world that can prepare you for the broken sleep that comes with raising a baby. Nothing. Despite it only being temporary, for the next five years or so, per child (I am not even kidding), it is certainly a shock to the system.

What we really need and want postpartum as mothers from our friends, family and visitors: help with our other kids. Not the baby.

The first month

Once you birth your baby, your solid night's sleep is a thing of the past, at least for the next few months or so. From birth until around three months it is normal for your baby to demand three- to four-hourly night feeds. I know, right? What the actual fuck. If you have a partner who takes some night feeds and is super helpful, bloody brilliant. If you have a partner who can't help overnight (like a lot of us), buy yourself an extra Gucci bag girlfriend because you deserve it. The truth is, if you are a breastfeeding mumma, dad unfortunately can't feed bub unless you give milk in the bottle. I feel like the earlier you accept this is your new norm, the easier it is. If you bottle feed, then absolutely utilise your partner. Some mothers, regardless of their method of feeding, prefer to do all the night feeds, while others appreciate the assistance of their partner with some overnight settling. Some partners get up with the mumma to assist overnight (with things like the nappy changes and heating milk) which is lovely, but also, in my eyes at least, kind of pointless. The way I see it, we need at least one well-rested parent, and if it can be you, *amazingggggg*, but let's be real, most mummas do the majority of the night work by themselves.

On this note I always like to think of the night feeds as my one-on-one time with bub, especially when I had more than one child in the house. With my fourth child, this is 100 per cent the case. I barely get to look at her during the day, so at night our time together is extra spesh. At least, I tell myself this anyway. I also acknowledge that during the night, when I am so mentally and physically exhausted, I am not alone – hundreds of thousands of mothers are up with me.

Remember how I mentioned earlier to take all the time to rest during the day? Like binge on your fave TV series? That is your time to catch up and 'rest' while you can. My morning cuppa is my saviour, and so is the moment I send my other kids off to school and childcare, *ha*! To reserve as much energy as possible for night feeds I suggest getting into bed at 7 pm or thereabouts when the baby goes down. If you already have kids at home, ignore this advice because I know it would be impossible unless you have unicorn kids who are down at seven and stay put until morning. Even if it means jumping into bed to watch TV, read a book, scroll social media or whatever, just lie horizontal as early as possible. This means your body is resting even if your eyes aren't.

I cannot believe I never took this advice on with Alfie. Oh wait, yes I can, because he never slept so what was the point of me attempting an early night, *ha*! Set realistic expectations of what lies ahead. I can guarantee that for the first few weeks at least, it is absolutely normal to expect two- to four-hourly night wakes. It is rough, but bub needs the calories and before long, hopefully by six weeks, they can give you much longer blocks, like five to six hours between feeds. Sounds like a dream, right? Keep reading to my sleepy time section in Chapter 9 and I promise it will be your baby in no time at all.

Loneliness

When I reached out to my social media audience to ask them about their observations on the fourth trimester, one experience rang out loud and clear – the loneliness that comes with having a baby. It is taboo. Unspoken about. We mums feel so selfish for experiencing this, yet so many do. What is it that makes us feel lonely during the fourth trimester? It's the emptiness we feel when baby is out. The quiet house during the day. The unspoken conversation we have with ourselves in our head. The lack of banter with our work colleagues. The kettle that doesn't talk back. The fridge that gives us nothing but cold milk. The dog that grimaces at us when we ask them a question. It's the car trips with the baby where the only noise you hear is the baby rattle and the annoying radio. It's the different conversations with your partner when they arrive home. It's the Maternal and Child Health visits with just you and baby, sitting with the other new mums in the waiting room as you all stare awkwardly at each other. All mothers feel it to a degree, yet don't talk about it out loud. Mothers are lonely when they shop for food, when they pram walk, when they cook, when they clean, when they nurse, when they try on new clothes, when they online shop and when they scroll their phone. I guess that's why we scroll so much.

Loneliness can also come from navigating this time mostly by yourself. No one to turn to for help. No one to answer your questions. No one to reassure you. No one to pull you out of your self-doubt. No one to 'hang' with. No one to talk to about your baby and partner. No one to share this rollercoaster with. At least it can feel this way, anyway. If only that village stood strong for us all. Despite it feeling overwhelming and lonely at times, those long days have beautiful moments too. First smiles, first giggles, first time rolling over, first tooth perhaps, first interaction with mumma and partner, and first time meeting new families in the same boat.

The long days also see you creating a wonderful bond with your baby, a unique one that no one else shares. Your baby becomes your new little bestie and despite not giving back in terms of conversation, they give you so much more in love and affection. They have a unique way of filling our hearts and souls and

The first month

making us forever grateful for these long days together that are tiring, yet so meaningful.

Intrusive thoughts

Why does no one ever warn us about this??? I learned the hard way, thinking I was losing my mind until I was told that intrusive thoughts are quite normal for new mums and, guess what, *so common* too. It's like it is almost a taboo topic. I remember mentioning it on my Instagram stories and instantly my inbox was full of responses from mothers – 'OMG ME TOO' . . . 'So it's not just me?' . . . 'YES why doesn't anyone talk about this?' . . . So here I am, talking about it.

See that kettle in your kitchen full of fresh boiling water? You might find yourself worrying that you could spill it on your baby. See that knife you are using to cut your carrots? Imagine if that accidentally stabbed your baby. You know those stairs in your house? How awful if you fell down them with baby in your arms. These thoughts are horrid and rude and inconvenient. They intrude into our brains and are completely unwanted. They can be the result of underlying anxiety, depression or OCD so it is important that if you do experience these negative intrusive thoughts that you visit your GP. Chances are you are simply one of the 50 per cent of mothers experiencing them, according to the Centre of Perinatal Excellence.

The most important thing is to understand you are not alone. I have been there, my sisters, my cousins, my besties, my patients too. Don't hide these thoughts or bury them, it will make them worse. Voice them to your nearest and dearest, and I can't stress enough, it doesn't hurt to check in with your GP as soon as you can, so they can reassure you everything is okay or help you manage any underlying mental health issues.

Phantom shower cries

Ugh, I hate to be the bearer of bad news, but these phantom cries will drive you mental. Literally.

Who would have thought a peaceful shower could turn into a scene from *Psycho*? One minute you are washing conditioner out of your hair and the next you are running from the shower, dripping wet to console your screaming newborn, who, in fact, was never screaming at all. I cannot tell you the number of times I have called Ambrose from the shower to plug baby's dummy or settle them only to be told they were actually sound asleep. You will get used to turning the shower on and off three hundred times in five minutes to check if the baby is crying. I'm not making this up.

The first month

Those phantom cries are so convincing, they will leave you scratching your head wondering if you need a psychiatric appointment to discuss the voices in your head. Just know, you aren't alone. We have all been left baffled by these ridiculously real noises that are in fact nothing at all. Hot tip: save yourself the anxiety and bring your monitor to the bathroom so you can enjoy your shower in peace.

As new parents (especially mummas) we are so hypervigilant that any sound we hear can feel urgent and distressing. Not to mention we are horribly sleep deprived. Obviously, if these phantom cries continue or worsen and consume your life, it is once again important to check in with your GP.

Monitor-checking obsession

To monitor or not to monitor, that is the question. Chances are, in this day and age, you will monitor. Our anxiety and need to snoop on our babies 24/7 while they hit the snooze button is real and I guess rightly so. We are so aware of the need for safe sleep that a monitor becomes a non-negotiable on the baby shower list. But do we really need to spend copious amounts of money on one? Do we need one that sings horrific lullabies? Should it come with arms so it can

---

Despite it feeling overwhelming and lonely at times, those long days have beautiful moments too. First smiles, first giggles, first time rolling over.

The first month

slap us to wake baby up? Absolutely not. All you need is one that has a screen, good range and adequate volume. You can avoid all the upsells and fancy bells and whistles many supposedly come with. And guess what? There is no shame in buying a second-hand one either. Heck, they often only get used for a few months before parents throw them down the hallway during the four-month sleep regression. Joking. Kind of. But seriously – don't overdo it. Just like the backpack for your first outing, small and simple is best.

Dealing with your partner

This is a tricky one. Another unspoken one. A real thing. The partner. The relationship. The changes. Mostly permanent. Perhaps for the better, or maybe for the worse. Nothing can prepare you for the changes your relationship faces when your baby is born into this world. The reality is, the partner now becomes second best, third at the finish line, last in your list of priorities, the third wheel. It's true and unfortunately we can't change that because naturally, that is just how it goes. You see the thing is, as hard as it is to admit, the freedom you once had together is now dominated by a baby that needs you, the mumma, more than they need the other parent, and organically, we mummas feel the same way. So how can your relationship change? In more ways than one.

One minute you are spooning each other in bed before baby arrives and the next minute the only spoons you are sharing are the dirty ones in the sink. One minute you are making a spontaneous dinner reservation for 8.30 pm and the next minute you realise it has been two years since you two had a date night. One minute you are binge-watching your favourite Netflix show together until 2 am and the next minute you are feeding on the couch in the early hours of the night all alone, no partner in sight. One minute you are debriefing about your day and the next minute you are talking to a baby that has no idea what you are saying and falls asleep listening to you babble. One minute you are holding hands on car trips together and the next you are rocking back and forth in the fetal position trying to pacify your screaming baby in the back seat. One minute you are walking the dog together and the next minute you are fighting over who takes the baby with them so you can have a twenty-minute reprieve between feeds. Life changes with the addition of a little one . . . it is that simple.

Your time together may be different, but it doesn't mean it's permanent or necessarily worse. Not only is your baby growing before your eyes, so are you both. Your hearts are bigger, your brain is expanding,

The first month

learning so many new things about life, and your waistlines may be a little larger too with all the take-away you have been snacking on instead of your once home-cooked meals. I feel like I fell more in love with each baby. A new birth somehow reignited our spark. Sure, we were tired and snappy as all buggery a lot of the time, but more than anything, there was this unspoken respect for each other. I was so proud that his body and genetics gave me my four incredible gifts, and him . . . well I don't know what he thought, but I know he liked me a little bit more with each baby we had. All in all, it changes, momentarily, and mostly for the better.

While on this topic, can I throw in the words 'couples counselling?' I was *never* going to be someone that engaged in these services because my relationship was 'so good' . . . that was until we had to learn to divide our time and manage a life with new additions. Couples counselling one trillion per cent saved my relationship. I was navigating two under two with Ambrose working a minimum of eighty hours a week and playing footy on top of that – you can understand when I say 'drowning' was an understatement. No one gets it until they are in this position. We fought, I nagged, he didn't get it . . . repeat. I wish hospitals would send couples home with a free five-session voucher to counselling because I don't think anything can prepare you for just how much your relationship and life in general changes once you bring a baby into the world. I am not saying it is worse, it is definitely more complicated and busy and expensive, but an outsider can really help you get your relationship back on track, understand your frustrations and assist in resolving them with unbiased solutions.

Check in with your partner

I know, right? Poor hubby or wifey. *Hello, hi how are you? I still love you, I do. I am just tired and exhausted and busy loving on the other half of my heart.* Check in with your partner. They may not be okay. They too are tired, overwhelmed, emotional, scared, defeated, excited, in love and, perhaps, feeling all the feels too. After all, they are the other half to this little baby so snug in your arms, and they may also miss you. They now must share you and didn't realise it would be harder than they thought. They understand that your new baby is innately your priority now and nobody else.

Speaking of checking in, has anyone debriefed with your partner post-birth? Are they okay seeing you cut open in order to bring your baby into the world? Are they traumatised watching you use every muscle and ounce of energy in your body, mind and soul to birth

The first month

your baby safely? Little things like this are often overlooked, and quite simply, they shouldn't be. Not just from a mumma point of view but from a midwife's, also. I consciously always make an effort to keep the partner informed during the labour/birthing process and, if possible, discuss the birth that was, the changes that happened, and how everything went down during the hospital stay. I wish there were more midwives available, or doctors had more time to debrief with the patients and their partners post-birth. It is just so damn important to an enjoyable postnatal period.

Up to one in ten new fathers experience some form of postnatal mental health problem. That statistic would be far greater if men were more open and educated on mental health, I believe. It's the damn stigma again that men can do it all post-birth, but the reality is, they simply can't and shouldn't have to. Postnatal anxiety and depression symptoms vary widely in fathers – they can be something as simple as not feeling confident caring for baby on their own (understandable too, which is why it can go undiagnosed) to suffering physical side effects like chest pain, panic attacks or a racing heart. Regardless of their mental health status (good or bad), it is important to communicate openly with your partner and provide as much TLC and reassurance to them as they hopefully have done for you. At the end of the day, if something doesn't sit right with you and you feel their mental health is off or they have changed, ask them to check in with their GP.

How partner can bond with baby

There is always the biggest song and dance made for mum and bub when baby is born. Like *der*, of course there is. Mum carried bub and birthed bub and now babe is relying on mumma (particularly if she's breastfeeding) to stay alive and grow bigger and stronger every single day. Partner often gets pushed aside (not intentionally) and is at the beck and call of our demands as a mumma, fumbling through each day during the fourth trimester doing what they can to appease us. But did you know there is *so* much they can be doing to fully immerse themselves in the whole fourth trimester experience and assist you as well? Not only will it support you, more importantly it gives them a chance to also bond with their newborn baby, providing them with some delicious oxytocin along the way, just like mumma gets. Partners will commonly say to us midwives, 'What can I do to help my partner – she is the only one that can feed the baby, I feel helpless.' There are so many ways a partner can be there for their baby. Something as small (though big to mumma) as doing the nappy changes, bathing baby,

One minute you are spooning each other in bed before baby arrives and the next minute the only spoons you are sharing are the dirty ones in the sink.

swaddling baby and settling them off to sleep, holding bub while mumma has a shower or takes a break, taking bub for a walk in the pram, massaging baby, cuddling and singing to bub during unsettled periods, especially witching hour, or even just talking to your bub. They know both parents' voices so well already from when they were in utero and partners will be pleasantly surprised how much they will be able to calm them, despite not having breastfeeding boobies readily available. If mumma is bottle feeding, partners can take turns in feeding the bottle too. Many partners, if mumma is breastfeeding, will opt to give the baby a dream feed at night-time, which is technically a rollover feed that bub gets late at night in the hopes they will sleep a longer block of sleep before the next feed. The dream feed is optional and if you are going to implement one I would encourage you to wait six to eight weeks until your milk supply has settled. I say, whatever works for your family. Essentially, the partner can actually do anything but breastfeed baby. Lucky them and their nips get a break, *ha*.

The doubt – what have I signed up for?

Having a baby can have us all fooled so easily. In the beginning it's all heart, eyes and love explosions, until one day it's just not. And then, out of nowhere, we question everything. The timing of it all. The capability. The skill set. The financial side. All of it. One day we are in love with our newborn and the next we may wake overwrought with doubt and guilt about our capacity to take on this new life requiring us to grow and nurture forever. It's too hard, we might think. It's not as enjoyable as we might have thought it would be. It's tedious. It's boring. It's damn tiring. I think the thing is, we as humans face this conundrum when we want something so damn badly and finally get it, we automatically doubt our capabilities and right to deserve such a blessing.

Birthing after a long time conceiving

Another thing that no one seems to talk about is when you finally birth your baby after a long time spent trying to conceive. As a midwife, I know infertility is rife and I see many, many patients walk into the birth suite or theatre excited but also damn afraid of what lies ahead. The disbelief that something they have prayed for for so long is about to enter their world. The relief that this time is almost over and baby is almost in their arms. The triumph of meeting their blessing, they are unaware it is perfectly normal to crash right back to reality once it has all happened. This moment they'd yearned for for so long perhaps does not feel as magical as they thought it would after all this time. None of this is unusual, but it is taboo and unspoken. Please know, if this is you and you didn't feel the 'high' of meeting your baby, you aren't alone and your feelings are so, so, so valid. Our minds can do freaky things to protect us and our hearts, so please, if this is you, always check in with your doctor, Maternal and Child Health nurse, midwife, friend, family or psych.

Social life post-baby

This is a hard one to write about because it is a bitter pill to swallow. And the thing is, you don't even realise it at the time, but your social life dramatically changes even before your baby has been born. It starts in pregnancy when you get the *can't be fucks* and you make excuses for cancelling dinner or an event. Then you have your baby shower and it's almost like a last hurrah, until you get yourself back together again months post-baby. Don't get me wrong . . . you will still see your friends, but there won't be benders or late-night cocktails. Instead, it will be interrupted coffee catch-ups or quick drop-ins between baby naps.

The first month

That's okay though . . . initially you won't be up for much more than that anyway.

On the days you are super exhausted or emotional you will miss your old life and your friends. You will mourn the days you were free to gallivant around the city streets without a baby attached to your titty and you will yearn for independent travel again . . . but it will come, in time. For now, you are where you are meant to be.

If your baby takes a bottle or you are a full-time bottle-feeding mumma this certainly allows you a lot more freedom when it comes to having time apart from your bub. Especially in terms of your social life. If you are focusing on the upside of bottle feeding, this is certainly one of them. If you are a breastfeeding mumma and you feel comfortable expressing so you can have some time off to meet with your friends, I highly encourage it. It is liberating having some time apart and enjoying yourself. I believe it is mentally important to try to enjoy yourself outside of your home as much as you can.

Lord knows how easy it is to stay indoors and make excuses so you don't have to leave the house. I am many months postpartum baby number four right now and am finding it difficult to allocate even a night a month for a dinner with my friends, let alone a date night with Ambrose. But it won't be forever. I know I keep saying this, but it's true.

Mothers' group

Arch nemesis or saving grace ... you decide! Personally, I think they are brilliant if you find the right match. Plenty report feeling isolated because their baby was the only one not sleeping or the only baby to bottle feed but I really hope you feel nothing but supported and included. I feel like the ideal mothers' group is a collection of women who band together for a giggle and cry at the week that was. Immunisations, broken sleep, appointments, arguments, stale food, messy homes, overflowing washing, too many visitors, first smiles, baby sleeping through, excellent weight gains, time to yourself and relaxing hair appointments. All these things matter and deserve to be shared with other like-minded mummas. I never joined a mothers' group. Not because I didn't want to, simply because my friends and I all had babies within a month or two of each other, so we made our own.

Is your baby too hot or cold?

Your baby needs socks ... Your baby needs a hat on ... You should strip your baby off in this heat ... Your baby looks cold ... I bet your baby has eczema from overheating her ... How about you all just fuck off with

The first month

your opinions and let me regulate my baby's temperature by myself!! This is one of the *many* annoying things you will have to deal with when having a baby. Every Tom, Dick and Harry has an opinion on absolutely everything and it is all uncalled for.

Knowing if your baby is hot or cold is easy to work out, and guess what? *You* always know best. If you are cold, so is your baby ... probably a little more so. If it is winter and you have a jumper on, your baby will need the same, plus an added layer. If you are hot and need a singlet, your baby needs a t-shirt. If you are cold at night and need an extra doona, your baby will need an extra blanket too. If they are sweating, take a layer or two off. If they are mottled and irritable, they are probably cold. Another way to check if your babe is at the right temp (apart from using a thermometer) is to place your hand down their back – if they feel warm to touch they probably are. If they are cool to touch, they are cold.

Another thing to note – when it is a hot day or your baby is in a warmer environment, they will more than likely need additional feeds. It is not uncommon for babies to demand further feeds during these periods and it's essential we meet their demands.

One thing is for sure, overheating our babies can be *superrrrr* dangerous so try to be as sensible as you can with this. It extends beyond their clothing – this means their environment too. Common sense isn't so common these days unfortunately, but trust your instincts always. Keep it simple. A safe room temperature for a baby to sleep in is approximately eighteen to twenty-two degrees.

CHAPTER 8

Survival mode – the first three months

It can be a lonely place, this world of motherhood. Especially if you are entering it for the first time. Nonetheless, let's not accept it as being this way. Let's shout from the rooftops that we need all the help we can get from our village to sail through it as smoothly as possible. While the fourth trimester is joyful, it is also challenging and you really are in survival mode. I will tell you why.

We aren't just surviving ourselves out there in the wild, wild west, we are ensuring our babies are surviving too. Surviving and thriving is what we are all doing in the fourth trimester. Our goal as mothers during this period is to ensure our babies are fed, gaining weight, bonding with us, meeting milestones, sleeping, learning and feeling content. Now that, my friend, is exhausting. How hard is it to keep ourselves treading water every day, let alone another human. This is why the fourth trimester is all about us mothers, our baby and nobody else. The start will be exhilarating, as I have mentioned, but once the adrenaline wears out, so do we. It is vital that during this period we and our young are our priority. Always.

All of a sudden the cute night feeds turn into a longer slog, and day breaks before we are ready. How can the night be over already? Survival mode I tell you.

Remember that time you slept in until 9 am after a solid ten hours sleep? It was beautiful, wasn't it? Now you may sleep in until 9 am but it comes after five wake-ups overnight, with a sum total of five hours broken sleep. How are we meant to function off that? There is only so much caffeine can do for us. Your Mondays become your Thursdays and your weekend becomes your weekday. Because it's all the same. Groundhog day essentially.

Some mornings you will bounce out of bed and other mornings you will curl under the doona and beg

Our goal as mothers during this period is to ensure our babies are fed, gaining weight, bonding with us, meeting milestones, sleeping, learning and feeling content. Now that, my friend, is exhausting.

for forgiveness for choosing this life. *Ha.* Not really, but some mornings are rough. Here are some of my suggestions to make this transition a little smoother.

- Get your food shopping delivered. That is a non-negotiable. Get a dinner delivery service like Hello Fresh or whatever is trending that month. That way your partner, or even you, can do the cooking, and it's much more convenient, quicker and often more cost effective.
- Walk every day. Even five minutes. Even if only up and down your driveway if you have had a caesarean section.
- Choose your visitors wisely. You don't have time to be emotionally drained by someone who doesn't draw breath.
- *Take* the help. And all of it.
- Sit in the sun. Vitamin D is deliriously underrated.
- Have a long shower every day. Sit at the bottom and do nothing but debrief with yourself over the day that was.
- Get into bed early. Even if you flick the TV on and watch it with your eyes shut, it's vital to rest up when you can.
- Online shop. Treat yourself. If you can't make it to the shops yet, for goodness' sake buy yourself

a non-pregnant piece of clothing. It feels good to do that.
- Get your hair done. With or without baby. Ideally without. This is your chance to sit for at least two hours all by yourself in peace. Don't feel guilty about it either. If you are breastfeeding, your boobs can be pumped and a bottle can be given. If you are bottle feeding, enjoy the freedom! It's important not to lose yourself too much in the thick of it. Sometimes you need that gentle reminder.

The six-week check-up

Many mothers seem to feel like the six-week check-up marks the end of their fourth trimester as essentially they say goodbye to their care provider until the next pregnancy, but it really isn't. You are actually only half way into your fourth trimester. The six-week check-up also feels like you have hit a milestone and congrats to you, because you have! Do you realise you have officially cared for your baby on your own without your doctor or midwife for the last six weeks? You should be bloody proud.

Your six-week check-up will either see you strolling into your obstetrician's office for the last time (until the next baby – *wink wink*), or, if you were a public patient like most of the country is, you will see your GP. Leaving this check-up can feel a little like a break-up – it's actually gut-wrenching leaving your ob. To feel so cared for and secure for the last nine months and to now have to care for yourself again is a bitter pill to swallow, but onwards and upwards with a hop, skip and a jump. You will walk away with a script or advice for contraception and a big fat world of gratitude. The appointment touches on everything from your birth, to any complications, to how you are currently feeling, to your healing process as well as checking in with your mental health and addressing any concerns you may have. At this visit your GP can check that your caesarean wound is healing, check your perineum is healing if affected, discuss any breast or feeding concerns, attend to any pap smears should they be due (cruel but lifesaving), answer any bladder/bowel issues you may be having and also try to rectify any overall health concerns, for example, thyroid, diabetes, iron deficiency issues. Basically, they want to ensure your health is optimal and you can get back to feeling your best. They may also request you do a follow-up blood test to check all your lovely levels (hello anaemia) and discuss a review in a few weeks' time if they feel it's required. They will throw the word 'intercourse' around and advise about contraception so your uterus has a well-deserved break. But it doesn't stop there. Your little baby too will meet their new GP for the first time and have a baby check if they haven't already had one with their paediatrician. How clever are our GPs? They will check bub's heart, their chest, their umbilical button, weight, their eyes, their fontanelle and address any concerns or red flags you have. Most mums leave their appointment with a weight off their shoulders as they have finally addressed everything they have had on rotation in their head for the last six weeks.

Sex

I felt you shudder from here. You either can't stop thinking about it or it's the furthest thing from your mind. I dare say if you are breastfeeding, you would rather cut your hand off than consummate your relationship again thanks to your hormones making your vjj as dry as the Sahara Desert, or maybe I am wrong.

Firstly, this whole waiting for six weeks thing is 'kind of' a myth. If you don't want your partner to know this, don't let them read this book. Basically, the whole six-week wait is to give your pelvic floor, vagina and cervix time to recover, as well as to avoid infection. Also – you could still be running the red river, but whatevs, *if* you feel well enough (go you, if you do) and there are no complications down there, you can absolutely resume intimacy once again. Will it hurt? The million-dollar question. Maybe . . . probably . . . not entirely sure. If it does, you wouldn't be alone, but it may be a sign to give it more time to heal.

Sex postpartum is similar to losing your virginity again. You are nervous, it doesn't feel amazing (yet) and it's just a little awkies. I'd say a lot of the time we kind of do it to just tick it off and get the monkey off our back. Don't get me wrong, there are some women, many women, who feel well and truly ready to go a few weeks post-baby and you get it *gurllll* if that's you. Sometimes, our partners aren't even ready. Unless you are Ambrose, he is always ready. I am not even joking. Some partners don't want to rush us, are scared they will hurt us, fear what our vaginas look and feel like, and some, if we are still bleeding, are absolutely repulsed by this idea. Give them time. Give yourself time.

Will your sex life be the same as before kids? I don't know. I feel like nothing is the same after you have kids. That might sound morbid, but I really believe it's true. Think about it, before kids, our bodies were internally physically unchanged. We had time. *Alllllll* the god damn time in the world to do what we wanted. We could sleep in and have sex. We didn't have babies waking us with their cry or little toddlers running into the bed. We could have late night sex. We weren't tired then. We also had more of a life. Freedom. The mental capacity to take it on. Dare I say it, we probably liked our bodies more then too. There are so many factors influencing you resuming your sexual relationship. What I will say is that I believe intimacy is a big part of a relationship and I believe it positively impacts both partners. It can give us mums a sense of feeling loved, connected, in tune with our partner and likewise for them. I know for Ambrose and me, it definitely makes our relationship stronger. There is less fighting, less friction, less whingeing from him, fewer expectations from me. It works for both parties. It can also make your partner feel like they are a priority again because, let's be honest, our babies are our number one priority forever and always once they are born. Bible. Fact. Truth. But in all seriousness, don't rush the sex, despite its importance. And for heaven's sake, when you do decide the time is right, use contraception, because guess what? Irish twins are a *realllll* thing.

Mental health

I could write a book on this topic alone. Where to begin? Your mental health and your partner's is just as important as keeping the baby alive. If you can't look after yourself then how can you be expected to look after a baby? It is that simple. The problem with mental health is the stigma surrounding it and the lack of support and resources accompanying a diagnosis of postnatal anxiety and/or depression. Maternal and Child Health nurses will do their best to detect any mental health issues, but it also comes down to your honesty. Our GPs should be good at managing our mental health but unfortunately aren't always, so it is easier said than done.

The reality is, we live in such a fast-paced, high-pressure, expensive, stress-filled world that it's no wonder mental health issues are on the rise. Times have changed. Mothers don't get adequate time in hospital to recover and learn the basic ropes of mothercraft; women are legit thrown out of hospital sometimes as soon as six hours post-birth and are expected to know how to breastfeed and keep themselves and their babies alive. We get thrown the excuses of bed shortages and lack of skilled midwives and nurses, but I can't help wondering where we have gone wrong. Our parents, forty years or so ago, got an average of five to ten days in hospital. Even in the public system! Now it's, *Cool here is your baby, the conveyor belt doesn't stop moving, pack your bags and get out.* No wonder our breastfeeding rates have declined and postnatal depression and postnatal anxiety rates have increased.

I wish our government paid for
and allowed our mothers to
spend a good week in hospital
to learn the basics of rest and
breastfeeding post-birth.

The Fourth Trimester

Maternity leave: don't get me started. What maternity leave? It's rubbish here in Australia. Cool, have your baby, spend a few short months at home, take this pay which will get you through five packets of biscuits and don't forget you need to go back to work full time to support the ridiculously big childcare bills you'll now have, not to mention mortgage or rent. Seriously, though, how are we meant to breathe? The pressure is insane.

I want to share some of my mental health journey post-birth to highlight some of these issues. Long story short, I was an experienced midwife having her first baby. I could settle any baby on the ward, attach any baby to the breast for a wonderful breastfeed and I could confidently reassure any worried new parent that everything was going to be okay. Then I had my baby. He breastfed like a champ but never slept. And I mean never from day dot. Me, the midwife, the maternal one, couldn't settle her own baby. I felt hopeless. I wasn't diagnosed with postnatal depression or postnatal anxiety, but I could feel it coming if I didn't get more than an hour and a half of straight sleep. So off we went to sleep school where I graduated with a new baby and an entirely new outlook on motherhood. Attending sleep school was the best decision I ever made. I was rested, mentally well and relieved I had help. If you are suffering from similar

Survival mode – the first three months

sleep-related issues, talk to your GP. They can supply a referral, which is required, to visit a sleep school with your baby.

Twelve months later I was pregnant with my second. This wasn't in my plans at this point, but it turns out the sperm couldn't wait and neither could my egg. It was a hard pregnancy. I could feel the pressure of having two under two, months off it becoming my reality. Lo and behold, my second was born and I became a mother to a newborn and a twenty-month-old who was a cyclone. Who didn't sit still. Who cried if he wasn't outside playing on the road with his trucks and dirt. I had a partner who worked six days a week, twelve-plus-hour days. I was spent, and each day I could feel the anxiety bubbling away but 'pushed' through. It was a hard first six months. Lack of sleep that crept in again, crazy hormones that struggled to settle, and a relationship that was falling to shit was a wonderful combination to concoct the world's worst postnatal anxiety, finally diagnosed and treated at nine months postpartum with my second child. It was fucked to say the least. But we came out the other side and life was good once again. I can't even explain to you how much anxiety affects your everyday life as a mother. I am grateful I didn't also have postnatal depression as I can only imagine how distressing that would be; my anxiety already felt like

The Fourth Trimester

it consumed every corner of my life. I had a brilliant GP who didn't take no for an answer and knew her shit, and a psychologist who turned my wheel back to straight and sent me on the right road ahead. I had the best family who acknowledged what I needed, and I was given time to rest, relax, recharge and steer things in the right direction again. But not everyone has this help. Not everyone is this supported. And it breaks my heart.

I don't have the answers, but I do wish this: I wish our government paid for and allowed our mothers to spend a good week in hospital to learn the basics of rest and breastfeeding post-birth. I wish our mothers were supported and not shamed if they choose to bottle feed. I wish we had postnatal visits every week at home for the first few months. I wish we had free access to sleep and settling classes, or even a week-stay program to help our tired eyes and bodies out. I wish we didn't have to return to work so quickly. I wish more funding was allocated to allow new mums to comfortably afford to enjoy maternity leave instead of fearing whether we can do a food shop this week. I wish we all had someone to tell us everything is going to be okay. I wish we all had help. Lots of help. Lots of love. Lots of support. I wish we all had someone to genuinely check in on us each day. But not everyone is that fortunate. I wish that we all, including partners, had endless access to professional help when we need it most. One can dream and hope.

How can you help yourself? By being true and honest with yourself. Be the one to voice it if you aren't coping or don't feel right. Talk, talk, talk to anyone that will listen and, for the love of god, please see your GP if you can feel your mental health declining, because you certainly aren't the first to seek help, you aren't the last and you aren't alone. Sleep deprivation can royally fuck with your mental health and trigger post-natal anxiety and depression, so please always, always, always prioritise your mental health.

Hair loss

This is not a drill. Postpartum hair loss is savage. Even the thickest of manes suffer hair loss, and there are multiple reasons for it, but put simply, our bodies are being depleted of all the good stuff and a drop in oestrogen. The answer? It's not simple. Time mainly. Hair loss starts around three months postpartum and can last as long as you breastfeed your baby or take to replenishing the lost vitamins. Generally by six to twelve months you will see your receding hairline sprouting some new growth. In the interim, load up on your everyday vitamins during this time, hydrate, get regular haircuts to promote new growth, maintain a healthy diet, and avoid harsh chemicals and heat on your hair. One thing is certain: your hair will make a comeback. Right now, Ambrose and I are having a competition over who is more bald, and he has a shaved egg head. I am not far behind him.

Your new normal – groundhog day

Groundhog day kills my soul. It really kicks me in the guts and gets me down. No one loves a home day more than me, but seriously, after a few weeks I feel like headbutting a wall if I have to unpack the dishwasher again or continue listening to the clothes dryer in the laundry doing its noisy rotation. Firstly, as a mumma, home truly is where the heart is, right? I get it. But home can also be super triggering if you don't get beyond the four walls of your lounge room. This is where the isolating part of motherhood comes into play. You wake up with droopy tits and perhaps an attitude to match. You want to get out, but you are tired. You try to get out the door, but then baby shits out of their nappy, requiring a jumpsuit change and a top-to-toe bath! And then, what do you know? It is time for another breastfeed, and baby only wants to sleep in your arms, not the cot or

Survival mode – the first three months

the god damn pram (cue my previous suggestion to get out first thing in the morning). Within an hour of nursing baby to sleep on your sweaty chest while compressing your full bladder, Dr Phil graces us on the TV screen and we know it's almost day over. Legit. This is what happens to us mums. We wake up, we feed, we change, we try to be human, we fail, we sit, we get a sore back, we hold our breath in the hope our baby stays asleep, and then we scroll our phone for three hours and, holy fucking moly, it's suddenly witching hour and Uber Eats are sending us dinner discount codes. Can you tell I have been through this four long times?

So, how do we break the shit storm of groundhog day? We do something different. We pre-organise a lunch with friends who can muster the courage to leave the house with their babies and are prepared to rock them in their prams in a noisy café for an hour or so. Even better, we arrange a dinner without babies so we can enjoy a glass of wine and adult conversation for three hours. The point is we try. It is better to get out, noisy café and all, than to stay stuck on our lounge surrounded by the clutter of the house. One thing is for sure, each and every day you will start to see the light at the end of the *lonnnnng* tunnel. Some days are all-consuming and overwhelming, and other days you will have a pep in your step and feel confident

Talk, talk, talk to anyone who will listen and, for the love of god, please see your GP if you can feel your mental health declining.

enough to join a mumma fitness class, followed up by a random coffee out with your new-found friends.

Housebound

Even if you are the world's biggest introvert you will likely become tired of the four walls that constantly stare at you all day. It is really easy to fall into the trap of being stuck at home all day with your baby. There is nothing wrong with it, until it becomes all day every day and then suddenly life feels super hard and your anxiety starts to creep in, because you haven't smelled the roses and breathed the fresh, crisp air in a few days.

Rest assured, there is no way in hell I am forcing you to commit to doing a class or scheduled activity outside of your house each and every day, but from experience, I am telling you that you will feel like a new person *if* you manage to spend just five to ten minutes walking around the block each day. I swear by it. It is *so* easy to blink and find the day is over, so if you pound the pavement, even at snail's pace, it does the world of good for you and your baby. Fresh air, some vitamin D, light exercise – all of it is amazing. Your mental health, heart and bones will thank you for it. Not to mention it makes you feel like you have achieved something for the day, and that, as a mum in the fourth trimester, is bloody unbelievable because sometimes we incidentally feel worthless (if you know, you know).

Exercise

Exercise, exercise, where art thou exercise? There is no doubt about it that intense exercise should take a back seat for the initial twelve weeks or so postpartum; however, this is always up to your own discretion. You need to be mindful that despite you perhaps feeling physically great and ready to step back into it, your internal organs and pelvic floor may require a much longer time to heal. This might mean you should rest more before beginning exercise or start back at a very basic level (despite how fit you may have been before your pregnancy), which is totally normal and to be expected. The best thing you can do prior to resuming any physical exercise postpartum is to visit your local women's health physio. They will be able to assess your recovery and how you are healing, and advise when and how to resume your exercise regime.

Personally, I believe, whatever your fitness level prior to conceiving or during your pregnancy, a gentle workout never hurt anyone. A short, slow walk in the first week if you feel well enough is not only beneficial for your physical health but may greatly assist your mental health also. As I have emphasised, never underestimate the power of fresh air and a small walk around the block, but do not force yourself to exercise if you do not feel ready. A little trick to ensure you can get a few steps in, some vitamin D and fresh air is to do a small pram nap with bub during their nap time or if you both need to get out. You will feel *so* much better getting out and about a little, because god knows how crazy you can feel being locked indoors all day with a new bubba, especially if you are still being smashed with visitors.

Shutting out the outside noise – trusting your gut

There is this thing called 'mum intuition' and believe me – it's real. It is a total inner sanctum for you and bub. Only you know best. Mumma knows best, always. Trust your gut and shut out the outside noise.

Everyone from Aunt Gladys to Grandma Shirley, from Poppy Joe to mother-in-law Cheryl, *everyone* has an opinion and a whole lot of advice. Let me say this though: some advice, particularly from your own mother or mother-in-law (if you have a good relationship) can actually be quite wise and sensible. I really believe they can have valuable input and add a whole lot of calm to your chaos. I remember my mum saying to me when I was having a hard time getting Alfie to sleep and I felt like I couldn't have him nap anywhere but his own bed (I know, what an idiot I was), 'It's okay to go for a walk with him in the pram, he might fall asleep there.' Just the push and sensible advice I needed.

Unfortunately, with a lot of great advice comes some seriously unhelpful, anxiety-provoking rubbish. And this is when you need to reason with yourself and trust your gut. The same goes post-birth if you feel something isn't right with you and/or your baby. You are now your baby's advocate and will be for a very long time to come.

Being comfortable in your own skin

I don't even know why I am touching on this in the fourth trimester, because the word 'comfortable', full stop, seems so far away. I mean, our skin is so different right now. Stretched, thin, weak, fragile, marked, saggy... all of the above. We are pretty weak and feeble in general in the fourth trimester and the idea of our body feeling whole again seems impossibly distant. But is it really? Instead of getting comfortable

Survival mode – the first three months

in our new-found skin and postpartum body, we need to get comfortable with the idea that the first few months post-baby is our new norm and perhaps this time is about surviving as we are right now, instead of trying to be something we are not capable of being just yet. What I am getting at is being comfortable in your own skin post-birth, and it can take a long time. What I don't think we account for postpartum is how much we (dare I say it) despise our bodies? I get the whole 'love yourself, your body is incredible' *bla bla bla* stuff, because it is, but it doesn't take away from the fact we may not like our bodies postpartum. This is something that is never spoken about either, because how dare we shame our bodies after creating and giving birth to incredible life. But if you have ever had a tight tummy and it now looks like a jelly slushy, it can be a bitter pill to swallow. Not to mention the tiger stripes (good old stretchmarks) that we thought would fade after baby is born but are still there, red, hot and raring to go. Learning to love our fragile body as we recover can be hard, and that is okay to admit.

There is, of course, a whole other spectrum of mummas that I wish I could be more like – the women who absolutely adore their body post-birth and celebrate it from the rooftops. I too was proud of mine, I just didn't love it.

Only you know best. Mumma knows best, always. Trust your gut and shut out the outside noise.

Survival mode – the first three months

Appetite and postpartum nourishment

Eat all the cake. Drink all the cups of tea. Order all the Uber Eats. Accept all the free meals family and friends prepped for you. Order from all the food shops online, and don't feel one damn bit guilty for snacking on that chocolate at your 3 am feed, but also tend to your body with some nourishing food and snacks. Broths, vegetables, legumes, meat and protein is a great way to start. Us mummas do hard things, but keeping ourselves nourished and hydrated at all times is one of the harder things to achieve postpartum. Do you want to know why? Because we put our babies before ourselves. It will be this way forever, actually. We feed them first. We eat last. We are their food and their water. And while they are drinking and eating away we are depleting ourselves without realising. Ensure your water bottle is full at all times. Breastfeeding makes you damn thirsty and plenty of hydration can increase you milk supply, which is a bonus too. Makes sense though. The more fluid you put into your body, the more fluid (milk) you make. Win, win! The best advice I have is to select *seven* healthy-ish meals that you can cook on repeat, that freeze well and that your partner can reheat, and just churn these out weekly. My staples are always a shepherd's pie loaded with veg; spag bol sauce full of veg and lentils; risotto (always freezes well); lasagna (lasts days in the fridge); different soups that are easy to defrost; and a good old stew or curry (not spicy of course). Ensure they are nutrient-dense foods so you can balance your sugar cravings, *ha*, and be sure to throw in lots of protein because believe me, postpartum you will be *starvinggggg*. Include all the good stuff too like some calcium, iron, wheat . . . veggies, fruit, the works. Also, don't underestimate how delish a boiled egg is. Filling, good for you and keeps in the fridge a few days. Thanks for coming to my nutrition (under-qualified in this area) TED Talk.

Witching hour

This bloody hour (sadly, it is often longer) can be extremely triggering when you first experience it. Witching hour is a period in the afternoon/evening where your baby is upset, feeding regularly and overall hard to settle. It will have you second guessing every part of your mothering instinct and have you googling 'why the heck won't my baby settle' every afternoon. In short, your milk supply is fine. It is definitely lower in the late arvo each day, but not to worry, our little gremlins suck the life out of our boobies to bring the supply back to where it is meant to be.

Survival mode – the first three months

Witching hour can be torturous if you are new to it. I am a seasoned campaigner in the witching hour world and I have learned to surrender to this nightmare hour or two and sit my ass on the couch with a baby perched on my tit. If I have Tim Tams next to me, I can survive it, and if my partner is home, I can blitz through it because I palm off said unsettled gremlin to him while I pretend to be busy with something else in order to avoid having to *shooosh* for the ninety-ninth time that hour.

I will say, though, with each baby witching hour reared its ugly head less and less. Maybe it was because I already had a house full of kids screaming down the hallways and drowning out baby's witching hour misery, or perhaps it was because baby was entertained by someone other than my stinky, odour-filled body. I'm not quite sure. Nonetheless, my best tips to soothe this rocky sea are to have your dinner cooked in the morning, because there is no chance in hell that baby is going to let you grate carrot and stir that spag bol on the stove in the evening, and go for a walk during this period if you can be bothered. The streets have never called me so intensely than this evil time of day. Some other ways to get you through the temporary nuisance of witching hour are to baby wear with a super comfy baby carrier (if your back can tolerate it), have a hot bath together, watch Netflix and chill while baby guzzles the boob or bot bot, get out and about in the car, or simply have three other kids so they can parent during this time for you.

Just know that when you are at the end of your tether, the end of your three-hour-long breastfeed, it's almost over and you will live to fight another day.

And one last thing: there are these weird unicorn babies that make witching hour sound like a load of bullshit. These unicorn babies sleep the afternoon away. They *goo* and *gaa* on their playmats and let their mummas prance around the kitchen cooking big ass meals while they entertain themselves. If you happen to be a unicorn baby owner, don't tell your mother's group.

Tapping out

Oh my god . . . maybe it's because I am four kids deep now . . . but this is definitely a thing. I remember in the early days of sleep deprivation, when witching hour paid me a visit for the first time, I was ready to tap the hell out by 3 pm. I would watch the clock with anxiety . . . following the little hand, *tick, tick, tick*, desperate for it to hit 5 pm because I knew it was bath and bedtime soon, and Ambrose would be home to take over the role of my empty tit. I would offload

Survival mode – the first three months

this gorgeous creature as soon as I could and usher Ambrose outside to take him for a walk so I could get ten minutes reprieve to shower myself before it became groundhog night. It was a small window of time that I needed solely to myself for myself to regroup and simply take a deep breath. You know, like coming up for air for the first time that day.

I highly recommend taking a solid fifteen minutes (at least) to yourself when your partner comes home for the night. If it means having a hot shower by yourself, so be it. A slow walk around the block can do the trick too, or perhaps even resting on the couch while your partner does the bathtime routine. It has been a long day – you deserve and need it.

Nap trapped

If there is one thing that is a non-negotiable when on maternity leave, it is subscribing to every single streaming service possible. I am talking Netflix, Stan, Binge, Paramount, Apple TV, *all* of them. Budget for them, trust me they will be worth it. Do you know how much of your time is going to be spent nap trapped on the couch? Enough time to set yourself up with an esky, a snack plate and a million TV series to binge. You might also want to think about learning how to self-catheterise because pissing with a sleeping baby on your chest is bloody hard. Take this time of being trapped to rest yourself. You will need it more than you realise.

Maternity leave

Is there anything better than a maternity leave countdown? I remember so vividly working my last few shifts in the birth suite thinking, *Holy shit, this is going to be me soon*. The swollen ankles, the vag pressure, the haemorrhoids, the achy back were on their own countdown. Mentally I was already on mat leave a few weeks before it officially started, and I am pretty sure the same goes for every single mumma nearing the start of their maternity leave.

For most it is the best time ever, to be clocking off for the last time, hopefully for a minimum of twelve months. But for others it can cause a lot of apprehension. Some mothers are absolutely married to their job, so the uncertainty of breaking up their work marriage to let another person into their life can seem super daunting. Not to mention upsetting the apple cart of the everyday routine they might be so used to as well. The financial unknown is also a reality check when you begin maternity leave. The bills won't pay

Survival mode – the first three months

themselves and life right now is more expensive than ever. Bills and money aside, I do hope you are blessed with a financially abundant time off, because how cruel not to be able to enjoy this wonderful time with our babies.

For me, I only took maternity leave after having Alfie. It was the best and hardest time of my life. It was mundane at times but gosh I hated parting with him, so I didn't rush back to work when I didn't have to. That being said, returning to work ended up making me a better mumma as I got to do my other favourite thing – help mummas and their partners bring their new babies into the world (and also have a cuppa with my gorgeous midwife colleagues).

Prior to going back to work after having Alfie, he and I would spend our time together like most other mummas. We would feed, have day sleeps at home, run some errands, attend appointments, hang at nanny's house, shop, see friends and be an old-school home-maker, *ha*! With my subsequent babes I never really took maternity leave. After bringing Essie home from hospital, I was back doing my in-home sleep consults by week three. I had clients around the clock. Owning your own business is no joke. It was much the same with Coco and Scout, only by this time I had a good team behind me. But I still worked more than ever.

My best advice to you is don't rush back to work if

I am a seasoned campaigner
in the witching hour world and
I have learned to surrender to
this nightmare hour or two
and sit my ass on the couch
with a baby perched on my tit.

Survival mode – the first three months

you don't have to. Time goes so quickly. Blink and you are walking them into primary school. Take your time together. After all, you are both growing up as one.

Going back to work post-baby

Can you believe I even have to put this topic into a book on the fourth trimester? Like, are we really talking about returning to work already? For real? If you choose to go back to work in the fourth trimester, you are a trooper. Or perhaps a little cray, like me. I never understood why women choose to return to work so soon if they don't have to, but as I grow older and wiser – *ha* – I have come to realise it is more than likely because they feel they are losing their identity, and I can definitely relate, having barely had any time off with my babes.

Paid maternity leave is usually so short, and life these days is so expensive, we now find ourselves heading back to the office earlier than ever, dropping our babies at childcare and slogging it out day in, day out just to make ends meet. Hardly seems fair, does it? If I had it my way we would offer every new parent a solid year off on full pay in order to care for themselves and bub. Enabling them to be really immersed in the new world of raising babies like they so deserve.

The Fourth Trimester

If you find yourself getting closer and closer to your return-to-work date, and are wondering how you are going to juggle it all and the change in routine once again, the first thing to solidify is who's going to care for your babe while you re-enter the workforce and make some cashola. Many utilise childcare and will have their baby transitioned there before they go back to work; others leave them with family members, perhaps making it easier on both of them to transition apart for a day's work; and others may hire a nanny. Another thing to consider is how to align your breast-feeds and/or pumping if you are still feeding babe. *Ahhhhh*, so much thought goes into parting with our little ones. More than we realise and can entirely prepare for in advance. We kind of find our feet along the way. Overall, I think one of the biggest struggles is finding the time to cook dinner, spend enough time with baby before they go to bed for the night, and fit in all your home duties that you missed out on during the day. Resorting to meal-prep options or Uber Eats is totally normal on these busy days, but this is for sure, the washing can always wait. Just like the rest of the fourth trimester – it's all about survival of the fittest.

Survival mode – the first three months

Time goes quickly

Time goes so quickly, they say, but does it? If you are relishing your role as a mother, absolutely loving the chaos and joy that this gorgeous baby brings, then no doubt you blink and it's their first birthday. But what if you aren't loving it? What if it all feels too much? What if the days feel so long you pray to wake up and find your life has been fast forwarded six months to an 'easier' stage? I know many women who despised the newborn period. Who dread doing it again. Who faced many challenges they weren't prepared for. There are *so* many variations in the postpartum experience and in the expectations you have entering it. One thing that is almost certain, if I can be so frank (again), is that you won't spring out of bed to start your day on the right foot every time. You will more than likely stumble out of bed unwillingly and start it on the left foot with a rolled up pooey nappy next to your bed. This season of motherhood looks different for everyone, and every day will bring a new feeling or experience.

CHAPTER 9

Sleep and settling

Strap yourself in . . . this is a *loooooooong* one, but such an important topic – I know you will come back and refer to this chapter regularly. Firstly, everyone will have something to say about newborn sleep. Some will try to jam a routine down your throat to implement from day one, warning you that to do otherwise will turn your baby into the world's worst sleeper. Others will tell you attachment parenting and co-sleeping is a necessity in today's world, which is also, *ahhh*, not true. *You* do *you*. You will find what works for you and your baby, and eventually get into your groove, but in the interim, I am going to share the basics, the 101, the bom diggity, the easy, the best, the most simple yet effective sleep wisdom I swear by. It goes something like this . . .

Swaddling

If there is one (other) thing I would shout from the rooftops as a midwife, mother and sleep consultant, it would be to swaddle (tightly wrap your baby like a snug burrito) your baby when they are sleeping from day one. They are born with the startle reflex which does just that, startles them if they aren't nice and snug. Swaddling is *so* soothing for your little one. Not only does it instantly calm them and make them feel safe and secure, it also mimics how they were in the womb. Warm and compact. Ask your midwife for a swaddling demo if you feel you aren't sure as it can certainly take some practice.

Awake time

I am not a stickler for any rules or routines when it comes to your baby's sleep in the first month or two of their life, *but* two things I strongly recommend following are their awake times and tired signs. Let's start with awake time, otherwise known as the awake

Sleep and settling

window. For a newborn baby, when we talk about their awake time, this includes their time feeding, the nappy change, burping, settling and swaddling before they go down for their next sleep again (even though it feels they just sleep their days away in the first few weeks). A newborn baby's normal awake time is generally forty-five to sixty minutes before they need to go down for another sleep. I know what you are thinking: *Whattttt? How can you possibly achieve all of that in that time?* Well, trust me, you can. And it isn't too strenuous either. We follow the feed, play, sleep pattern. More on that in a second. Why are their awake windows so small? They tire *so* easily at this age. Feeding is like running a marathon to them, all that suckling, guzzling, digesting – it is beyond exhausting for babies. When they wake up (or you wake them), you unswaddle them, place them on the breast or give a bottle and try to have a good solid feed each time. Now, we all know a breastfeed takes longer than a bottle feed so please don't cut them off if your feed is nearing the 45-minute mark as this is to be expected and normal for this age. Breastfeed/bottle feed, burp, nappy change, re-swaddle and put them back to bed. The thing with babies is we tend to overcomplicate things when we don't have to. All you need to know is that newborn babies get over-stimulated easily, tire quickly and take in more milk then we realise at each feed.

I am not a stickler for any rules or routines when it comes to your baby's sleep in the first month or two of their life.

Sleep and settling

Baby sleep cycles

A baby sleeps in very different sleep cycles to an adult, for the first few months anyway. They spend more time asleep than awake in the first three months of life, and from there, their sleep cycles drastically change. Instead of spending the majority of their sleep cycle in REM and non-REM sleep, they all of a sudden mimic an adult's sleep cycle of four stages (hello, four-month regression incoming). Sounds complicated right, but it's actually not. This is why I really encourage parents to enjoy lots of baby snugs in the fourth trimester (and forever of course), because after the first few months, sleep can be a little challenging at times.

Routines

The word 'routine' can be so anxiety provoking in the fourth trimester. Almost like an extra bit of pressure we may feel on top of an already giant to-do list. However, ironically, this is what many families and babies crave very early on in the piece. Predictability. Our babies are creatures of habit. Even in the womb they tend to have their own little routine. Drink your liquor (amniotic fluid), wriggle about, wee, sleep, repeat. The truth is, if you are aiming for a well-rested, settled baby that feeds and sleeps well, often a routine will achieve this. Now, let me preface this by saying I have never in my nine years of parenting had a strict routine ever, but that is just me. Early on I would definitely not encourage a strict one, anyway. I have always been a more relaxed 'follow your baby's lead'-type mumma, which saw them feeding and sleeping around the same time of day anyway. They tend to put themselves into their own natural routine according to their body clock.

Routine also depends on the type of person you are. Some (many) are very meticulous and like to do the same thing at the same time in their daily schedule, and while that sounds great, it is not always achievable when it comes to our babies.

If you ask me as a midwife and sleep consultant what a newborn routine should look like, I will tell you to feed on demand, bathe at the same time every night and put baby to bed around the same time every night. Something as gentle as this can be enough to guide your baby to achieve wonderful sleep habits.

Obviously, as they grow older their needs and wants will change, and therefore so does their routine. When the fourth trimester comes to an end is often the period when parents like to create a bit of a firmer, more predictable routine, and I agree, for this age, they genuinely thrive off that.

I always bang on about our babies not being robots,

Sleep and settling

but it is so, so, so true. Mostly, they adapt super well to any changes you might like to make in their daily routine, but also be mindful, sometimes we just need to go with the flow.

Safe sleeping

I am not going to lie, safe sleeping plays on my mind regularly as a mother of four, even when I know they are sleeping safely. The idea that SIDS (sudden infant death syndrome) can still occur despite our best efforts as parents to provide the correct sleep environment absolutely devastates me. It causes immense anxiety for me personally, and still to this day, when my babies have a big, long block of sleep, I wake absolutely freaking out. It must be the innate maternal instincts in us or the fact that SIDS is a reality for many families, but whatever, whenever, whoever, please, please, please educate yourself on safe sleeping before you give birth, after you have given birth and when you go home. There are so many things you can do and steps you can take to ensure your baby is sleeping safely, so it is extremely important you always follow the Red Nose guidelines, which you can find at rednose.org.au. One of the most important things to note is to ensure your baby is put to sleep on a flat surface with nothing that can potentially suffocate or harm them, and to allow adequate air flow. Please please please always keep up to date with safe sleeping guidelines.

Night one

Your baby will more than likely give you a big chunky block of sleep, say four to five hours, and you will be asking yourself how you got a unicorn baby. You didn't. There are no unicorns here, just a tired baby after a hard day's work being born into the world. This big block is generally a one-off and is totally fine if the mother didn't have gestational diabetes or the baby wasn't born with any health conditions.

The reality is, their first feed is like running a marathon for them, as I've said. Their stomach can only take around 5 to 7 millilitres per feed, so this is *very* tiring, arduous work for them, requiring a snooze afterwards.

Your baby is also born saturated with your melatonin in their blood stream, which is a hormone that is produced in conjunction with darkness and is responsible for the body's circadian rhythm and internal body clock. On top of this, a newborn baby generally sleeps a minimum of sixteen hours over a 24-hour period. When they are awake – which is super brief, generally no longer than an hour at a time (and that is stretching

Sleep and settling

it) – they will spend it feeding, burping, grimacing and trying to settle back to sleep. It is *vital* that your baby is feeding at the breast or having bottle feeds on demand (when they request it) or at least every three hours in the first few weeks post-birth.

Night two

Chances are your birth adrenaline has worn off, your nips are a little tender and you as mumma are feeling exhausted, but your baby not so much. Have you ever heard about what happens night two post-birth? I swear, no one ever talks about this, but it is such a real, exhausting, headfuck of a thing. On night two, your little unicorn baby becomes a savage leech stuck to your tit pretty much for the whole night. And when I mean the whole night, I mean the whole night. Night two is when midwives find themselves assisting the most with feeding and settling, because all your baby wants to do is feed, feed, feed. Their itty-bitty tummy suddenly gets bigger and they get *hungryyyyyyyy*, desperate to bring your milk in. The most important thing you need to know is *this is normal*. There is nothing wrong with your baby and certainly nothing wrong with your breastmilk. All they are doing is trying to bring your milk in so they can feel nice and

The Fourth Trimester

full and content. You see, our breasts are so clever. They pretty much have their own brain. The more your baby is put to the breast and suckles away, the quicker your breasts begin to increase their volume of milk and expand in size. Whatever you do here, don't doubt your milk supply, there is nothing wrong with it, and your baby is doing exactly what it is meant to do – that is feed, feed, feed.

During this night, if your nips haven't had a minute's rest – coming from an experienced mumma's perspective, much to some people's dismay – the dummy, aka the pacifier (it has this name for a reason), can be a wonderful settling tool as long as you aren't using it to replace a breastfeed. I am talking if your baby has sucked like a hoover with no break in between and your nips are close to falling off, the dummy could give you and your breasts a moment of reprieve.

This night of constant cluster feeding generally lasts a night or two, so please enlist your partner or midwife if you are feeling exhausted or overwhelmed. Most of all, know you aren't alone. There are thousands of mummas up feeding around the clock with you right now, so we are all in it together.

If you are one of the lucky mummas who somehow manages to skip the night two clusterfeed, I am jealous . . . we all are. You too have a normal baby, and normal breastmilk as well.

Our babies are creatures of habit. Even in the womb they tend to have their own little routine.

Night three

You are either going to have a repeat of the night before, hopefully to a lesser degree, or you might be lucky enough to get a solid few hours of shut-eye before the baby wants to feed again. The reality with newborn babies is that once your breastmilk is fully 'in', feeding and settling will be much easier. You will notice it becomes a pattern of feeding your baby, them falling asleep at the breast, you changing their nappy, trying to feed again, swaddling them tightly (they love this) and then popping them down. Repeat this for the next few weeks.

Nights four to seven

Well done, you have successfully survived week one of f-all sleep and a sore, tender body. But you did it, you both did, and somehow sleep changes again and again and again for the next two years of their life at least, *ha*.

Week two

You will slowly be finding some sort of groove. Your milk will be well and truly in, and your baby may now

Sleep and settling

be unsettled from having so much of it that they have tummy pains. If so, you may start doubting everything all over again. I am making motherhood sound so damn glorious, aren't I? But no one is ever super honest about this stuff and how hard it can be.

Despite this, week two will find you falling into a little bit more of a rhythm in terms of feeding and sleep. You will learn that your baby settles well with a nice snug swaddle, and that they get so tired feeding they struggle to finish a feed. There is no need to create a routine yet (or at all), and it is imperative this time is spent together with lots of cuddles, skin-to-skin, bonding and feeding. It is such a fleeting period that you blink and it's over – the whole first year is – so try to surrender to the beautiful chaos that is now your new normal. With your milk establishing in abundance, or your little one downing their bottles, you should be able to get two- to four-hourly blocks of sleep at night and during the day.

Week three

This week you will see some significant changes with your newborn and their sleep. At three weeks of age they generally have their first big *growth spurt*, which means they will ramp up their feeding once again. No, there is nothing wrong with your supply, your milk is adequate, they naturally just demand more of it as they are doing lots of growing. If you are bottle feeding, they might demand more millilitres per feed, and this is super normal too.

Colic also peaks at week three, making for an interesting game of 'Guess Why My Baby is Crying Now'. A lot of extra feeds, development and colic are rolling into one right now.

On top of this, you will find your little one suddenly waking up to the world. Your once sleepy baby is now having more awake time and might perhaps like to sleep a lot of the day and party all night. You know, the typical 'baby having their days and nights mixed up' that we hear about so often. At night they want to play and engage and fuss and spend more time awake, and during the day they drift off deeply and we find ourselves waking them for a feed. *All* normal and common. So, what can you do to maximise night-time sleep and create a gentle structure for during the day? It is actually much simpler than you might think. Read on to learn how you can implement a touch of sleepy magic so you both get adequate zzz's throughout your day and night.

Dark room
At three weeks of age I strongly recommend sleeping your baby in a dark environment, whether that be in

Sleep and settling

your room or their own sleep environment. Remember I mentioned that in the first few days they are saturated with their mumma's melatonin hormone? Well now it is starting to wear off (hence they are more awake) and now it is up to their own bodies to make their melatonin, which is produced in response to a dark environment. For this age, it doesn't have to be a pitch-black room, but the darker the better. Essentially, do feeds in the daylight then walk into their dark environment and place them to sleep in their cot or bassinet tightly swaddled.

White noise/lullabies

When we place our babies into a dark room for all sleeps (night and day), I also recommend starting some white noise or lullabies/sleepy music at the same time. This white noise/sleepy music plays for the duration of their whole sleep (night and day) and doesn't stop until they wake up. Not only is the white noise/sleepy music naturally relaxing, it also creates a positive sleep association. It assists your baby to have longer and deeper periods of sleep. When you enter your baby's dark environment to put them to sleep, you simply switch their music on, place them on their back swaddled in their cot or bassinet to have their day nap or night-time sleep.

Week four

Congratulations!! You have been a mumma for one whole month . . . I bet it still feels like a dream . . . or perhaps reality is setting in faster than your body is bouncing back. On the topic of bodies – your little one is growing stronger and bigger every day. Catnapping might commence around now, or if you are fortunate enough, you may just get to hold onto your solid day naps a little bit longer. This week is pretty uneventful in terms of sleep. As you know, these first few weeks and months are all about bulking bub up and really immersing yourself in the newborn bubble.

Week five

You will be feeling more confident in your role as mumma to your little one. Some might say you are even growing a little cocky and ready to take on the shops all by yourself, with your wee babe and backpack loaded with baby essentials. Go you good thing. I am proud of you because that shit is hard. In fact, now really is a good time to trek to the shops or nanna's house or take on a tour of Australia in a week because that sweet spot of baby sleeping here, there and everywhere ends soon. I wish I took my own advice more and didn't sweat the small stuff in the early days of sleep when I didn't have to.

One last thing for week five. Enjoy this last week of long day sleeps because if it hasn't already, the catnapping will more than likely begin next week.

Week six

Woo hoo, week six. You have made it six whole weeks as a mumma bear! Six weeks of feeding, nappy changes, zombie sleep cycles, baby baths, a billion cups of coffee and, lately, a whole lot of baby resettling, right?

Ahhhh, here we are at the six-week mark, people seem to announce so jubilantly on their social media posts. I have no idea why. What on earth makes the six-week mark such a milestone anyway? Perhaps it is the first proper 'check-up' post-birth? Or the 'go ahead, you are free to fornicate once again' pass – which is a total crock of shit, by the way, because you can actually resume intercourse whenever you feel well enough. But let's not tell our partners that.

Maybe the hype around six weeks is that babe has their second big growth spurt and all of a sudden they turn into a cat. A catnapper that is. The dreaded catnapping. *Where has my dream sleeper gone?* Gone. They are now a cat. Napper. Say hello to 35- to 45-minute sleeps

---

Feed on demand, bathe at the same time every night and put baby to bed around the same time every night.

Sleep and settling

instead of those luxurious two hours of time to yourself. Will every baby catnap? No, but I really believe (no definitive stats here) that 99 per cent of babies go through a period of catnapping at least once between week three and eight. Some parents couldn't care less that their baby has super brief, sporadic naps because they feel like they can get out and about more now, whereas others – for example, me – break out in hives the second the clock hits forty-five minutes because they know five thousand per cent their baby will wake at that exact moment. All four of mine did. And it was annoying and frustrating and tiring and repetitive, but we pushed on, and I persisted with teaching them to link their sleep cycles again, which is such a fun skill to learn (eye roll big time here). Remember at week three I mentioned the dark room and sleepy music for every sleep? This is why. It is more important now than ever, and even better if you got a head start from week three. Not only will your baby be ready to party after their first sleep cycle, but they will also fool you that sleep is for the wicked and it's more fun to get them up and repeat the same thing sixty minutes later. Your baby needs sleep. And they definitely need more than the one sleep cycle they are accomplishing, but they will need your help to get them back on track. Will every baby learn to link cycles again? The short answer is no. Some babies, despite the dark rooms, the white noise, the positive sleep associations, the longer awake time, the shorter awake time, five sleep consults, five hundred google searches and never-ending settling, will just never sleep longer than one cycle at a time.

This week may also coincide with your baby's immunisations, so lots of cuddles, feeds and TLC are on the agenda for the few days following baby jabs.

Weeks six to twelve

Weeks six to twelve bring you a whole new world developmentally with bub. They begin social smiling, babbling and you may even get a little laugh soon. They will find their hands around now and spend a lot of their time sucking them and eventually reaching out to grab their toys. They seem much more playful and alert. Their awake time can be extended ever so slightly too.

Baby generally has their next lot of immunisations between week six to eight, so be mindful during this period not to expect too much in terms of sleep. They are often more unsettled, tender and sometimes even sleep more. I just say to follow their lead here. During weeks six to twelve they will be doing lots of growing, will start practising their rolling, trying to escape their swaddles and maybe even beginning to

Sleep and settling

protest naps and bedtime more. They will be familiar with what it means when you enter their room, *hello sleepy timeeeee*, and by week twelve may start waking up more frequently overnight. The joys. This is all leading up to the end of their fourth trimester and the start of the four-month regression. You have no doubt heard about this regression. It's a big one. In short, the four-month regression is a period of time where your baby's sleep may feel like it is going backwards, but in fact their development is going forward. During this time their sleep cycles become less 'baby like' (three- to four-hourly blocks) and more adult like (one- to two-hourly blocks). As a result, your little baby, who once gave you a decent block of sleep at night, may all of a sudden be waking every one to two hours overnight. This is no fun for anyone, but rest assured, not every baby's sleep will be affected, and if it is, this period of disrupted sleep should not last more than a few weeks.

The transition from swaddle to sleeping bag

If your baby is actively rolling (this generally happens between three to five months), you will need to make the transition from the swaddle to the arms-out sleeping bag. You can go two ways about this! Cold turkey (which I recommend) or a gradual transition of one arm out at a time, alternating one arm per nap over the course of a few days until both arms are out completely. If you go cold turkey they transition much quicker, but there might be a little more whingeing initially. It is totally up to you. The last thing we want or need is a rolling baby stuck on their stomach strapped in a swaddle. It is dangerous and not recommend by Red Nose guidelines. If your baby is not yet rolling, there is no need to unswaddle just yet.

The transition from bassinet to cot

This is a tricky one. I never recommend this unless baby is going into their own room (which is not recommended until six months, as per the Red Nose guidelines), or they are too big for their bassinet, there is no room and it is waking them. Very much like the arms-out approach, I recommend this cold turkey transition. Some people will opt to do day naps in the cot to begin with, then move onto their night sleep; however, I recommend once you are making the transition to their cot, all sleeps – day and night – now occur in this space. If you don't feel comfortable moving baby into a cot in their own room/sleep environment, there is no harm putting a cot in your bedroom if it fits, so you both feel more comfortable. This is up to your discretion; however, regardless of this, always follow up-to-date Red Nose guidelines.

CHAPTER 10

What we can learn from other countries

I firmly believe we Westerners could take a leaf out of how people in other countries navigate the fourth trimester. It is a period of such tremendous change, healing and bonding – why don't we treat it this way in Australia? Instead of wrapping ourselves up in our beds for up to forty days like they do in China and India, we make it a competition to see who can achieve their first five-kilometre walk with bub after birth. Insane if you ask me. Let's take a look at some of the traditions and practices common in other countries and see if we could learn a thing or two from them.

The Fourth Trimester

China: The Golden Month

The Golden Month says it all. Sounds dreamy right? Well, it is. In China, their postpartum period is known as *zuo yuezi* or 'sitting the month'. Australians of Chinese heritage sometimes practice this in Australia too, especially if a grandparent travels here from China for the birth and stays for many months afterwards. For an average of thirty to forty days, new mothers are encouraged to rest, stay warm, and avoid physical exertion (give me this any day of the week). Basically, stay put in bed where they focus on healing and bonding with their baby.

Family members maintain the chores of running a household while also nurturing mum with traditional postpartum meals such as chicken soup with ginger and dates, which is believed to help restore the mumma's energy and overall health.

This practice (which we should all emulate) allows mumma to completely recover, and bub to feed and grow in a slow, warm, loving environment.

India: The sacred forty days

Similar to China's Golden Month, India's postpartum period, referred to as *jaappa*, lasts approximately forty days. It is a female-dominant practice in which the new mother is cared for by her own mother or female relatives. Traditional Indian medicine (Ayurvedic)

What we can learn from other countries

plays a big part in the mother's recovery during the postnatal period – mumma indulges in well-deserved massage, yoga, acupuncture and herbal baths, and also follows a rich diet full of ghee, herbs and spices. This sacred period allows the mother to recover and bond deeply with her baby, away from the stresses of daily life. I bloody wish we all could enjoy something like this. How amazing would that be?

Latin America: La cuarentena

Many Latin American cultures similarly lap up a forty-day relaxion period. Their postpartum period is known as *la cuarentena*. During this time, new mothers are encouraged to rest, avoid strenuous activities and follow a specific diet to aid recovery. (Australia – are we taking notice of this???) Foods such as nourishing broths, oatmeal and herbal teas are commonly consumed. Family and community support is strong, with relatives often stepping in to help with household chores and childcare for older children. *La cuarentena* places strong emphasis on nurturing the mother's health and well-being and making her super strong again so she can care for her newborn. See what they do there? Caring for mumma first so she can take care of everyone else. Very much like the 'filling up one's cup' theory.

I am so down for this, and am especially impressed

We make it a competition to see who can achieve their first five-kilometre walk with bub after birth. Insane if you ask me.

with the 'taking care of the other kids' part. I think we *all* need a bit of this, more than anything. *Woweeeee*, go Latin America!

Malaysia: Pantang

The *pantang* period in Malaysia lasts around forty-four days. I am sure no one is complaining about this. It consists of heavenly body massages with warm oils, herbal baths and abdominal binding (not sure I would love this bit) to help mumma's body recover. They nourish mumma with warm drinks and food to give her strength and balance her energy, and I guess settle her hormones too. Once again there is little to no physical exertion for mumma, with a whole village of family members behind her caring for everything and everyone in the household. I think I want to move to Malaysia after reading about this.

The Netherlands: Kraamzorg

I am a massive rap for the Netherlands. Not only are they one of the world leaders in successful home births, they place a massive focus on postpartum healing and restoration. Their postnatal period is called *kraamzorg*. New mums are allocated a *kraamverzorgster* (maternity nurse) who does in-home visits post-birth. There is a special check-in visit every single day for eight days! Kind of like bringing your midwife home with you for a week, *ha*! The *kraamverzorgster* helps with baby care, breastfeeding and household tasks, providing invaluable support during the early days of motherhood. This practice ensures that new mothers receive professional care and guidance, promoting a healthy start for both mother and baby – something that every single family deserves. Should I send a copy of this book to the Australian government? I think so!

Nigeria: Omugwo
In Nigeria, particularly among the Igbo people, they have a postpartum tradition known as *omugwo*. New mothers are cared for by their own mothers or other female relatives who come to stay and assist with baby care and household chores while mumma gets some well-deserved rest. The new mother is encouraged to sleep and devour nourishing foods like pepper soup and yam (sounds interesting but nonetheless nutritious I am sure). This period allows the mother to recover and learn from the wisdom and experience of the older generation, fostering a strong sense of community and support which so many mummas in other countries lack.

Do you see what I mean? We in most Western countries are so behind the eight ball it isn't funny. Is it because we don't see the same value in restoring health as other countries do? Is it because we are too

What we can learn from other countries

independent and controlling? Is it because our babies' grandparents are probably still working full time at the time we have our kids? Or would we consider it as being too 'spoilt' to be granted such incredible help for the month post-baby? Whatever the reason, the demand for postnatal support is growing worldwide and it is no surprise. Women are burnt out. Lonely. Tired. Sore. Sleep deprived. And, more than anything, rush themselves to bounce back too quickly, which I believe is thanks to social media.

I legit feel, though, that perhaps maternal and paternal mental health problems wouldn't be so rife if we had the TLC and support we so desperately need after our babies are born. No wonder postpartum doulas are becoming more common, as they provide the physical and emotional support that new families need but don't otherwise have access to. Our postnatal birthing traditions may not be anything like China's or India's; however, there is an increasing appreciation of the importance of nurturing and caring for new mothers during this transformative time and awareness that we need back the 'village' that our older generation enjoyed years before us.

We can only dream and continue advocating for this. I guess it's the backbone to my business, constantly supporting fresh mummas straight out of the hospital bed and into their own.

Conclusion: When it is all so beautiful and not, rolled into one

The general consensus on motherhood is that there are more challenging times than easy ones, and I have to agree. This is the reason I have predominately been talking about the realities (which are the hard times) of motherhood. Don't get me wrong. It is so, so, so beautiful too. I have gone back for four, and perhaps have one more to go, so it can't all be too bad, but the fourth trimester for me, and for a lot of you too, appears to be a mini battlefield at times. The beautiful moments, though, always far outweigh the hard, bad times.

The love our children bring to our lives and those around us is like nothing we've ever experienced before. Surrender yourself to what is right for you and your family ... if your baby is happy, healthy and content, you are doing a phenomenal job. If your days are hard and you wake to face another day, you are killing it mumma. Sometimes you laugh, sometimes you cry. Sometimes you smile, sometimes you frown. Sometimes you nail it, sometimes you are chasing your tail. Sometimes you sleep, sometimes you don't. Sometimes you run, a lot of the time you walk. Your fourth trimester should be a period of grace, bonding and gratitude – after all, you have conceived a miracle, nurtured it to the end and birthed your biggest

What we can learn from other countries

blessing yet, even if it doesn't feel like that right now. Motherhood is nothing short of beautiful, yet hard, all rolled into one, and that is more than okay.

Motherhood is the most underpaid, underprepared, underrated, unbelievable, transformative time of your life. One day you are you, yourself and I, and the next minute you are carrying someone else in your heart, mind, body and soul for the rest of your being. Your DNA is now engrained in your child, forever and ever. Your life expands in more ways than one. Your goals, ideas, perspective and reality changes. Nothing is permanent. You have more fleeting thoughts than ever before. You learn new definitions for the word 'worry'. Your sleep is forever impaired. Broken, even until the teenage years grip you. Your relationship forever altered . . . maybe for the better, maybe for the worse.

There is nothing truer than the saying 'comparison is the thief of joy' when it comes to our children. Not one baby is the same as the next, and this is also true of ourselves as mothers. How can we possibly judge one another when our circumstances are so different? If we brought back our old-school village, had a lifetime supply of money and weren't forced to go back to work early due to the cost of living and pressure, I believe our postpartum experience would be so different and far more positive. In saying this, let this book be a reminder that we are really in it together, on our own journey and motherhood is not linear. I have now endured the fourth trimester on four occasions and each time has been so different. Lots of wonderful experiences and many not-so-joyous moments. As a woman, as a mother, as a friend, sister, daughter, partner, midwife, sleep consultant and lactation consultant, I say let's leave the judgement for another day. Or better yet, not at all. If we backed ourselves and each other, this world would be a much better place.

If you are having a rough day, I want you to refer back to this book. I want you to know I am holding your hand through it. You may not be having a good day, but it's just a bad day, not a bad life. You may be feeling alone; trust me, you aren't. When you are up feeding your baby in the middle of the night, know there are hundreds of thousands of mothers across the globe doing the same. When you are overwhelmed, think of me. No one has their shit less together than me. When you hate your partner, and your kids are being horrid, I am right there with you. It will get better. And when you are absolutely overjoyed with love and didn't think your heart could expand any more, believe me it will.

After the fourth trimester comes so many firsts. First tooth, first clap, first wave, first food, first birthday, first sleep through, first everything. Enjoy every day, even

What we can learn from other countries

the crap ones. They soon become a distant memory. The sleepless nights, the rough starts, the long days, the doubt – it all disappears, and before you know it, you will be ready to do it all again.

I wish your fourth trimester to be blessed with endless support, an abundance of love, an enriched relationship with your partner and new child, and a lifetime of good health and happiness. Until the next time, you have got this mumma. In it together.

Notes

Chapter 1: Ground zero: The birth

It is actually a little surprising if you think of birth as a natural event to consider that according to the Australian Institute of Health and Welfare the number of women having vaginal births has decreased and caesarean sections increased over the last decade or so: 'Australia's mothers and babies: Method of birth', Australian Institute of Health and Welfare, 13 December 2024.

In 2022, only a small portion of women in Australia (0.5 per cent) birthed at home safely with the assistance of a registered midwife: 'Australia's mothers and babies: Place of birth', Australian Institute of Health and Welfare, 13 December 2024.

In the UK the Office for National Statistics reported that in 2020, 2.4 per cent of women in England and Wales gave birth at home: 'Birth characteristics in England and Wales: 2020', Office for National Statistics (UK), 13 January 2022.

The Fourth Trimester

Statistics in Australia report one in three women have identified their birthing experience as traumatic; however, this does not mean it will necessarily be you: 'Inquiry into birth trauma', Perinatal Anxiety and Depression Australia (PANDA), 15 August 2023.

Chapter 2: The hours after the birth

The American College of Obstetricians and Gynecologists lists the benefits, particularly in preterm births, as being associated with the 'establishment of red blood cell volume', decreasing the potential need for blood transfusion, and also lowering the risk of nasty things such as your baby's gut tissue dying and bleeding on the brain: 'ACOG recommends delayed umbilical cord clamping for all healthy infants', American College of Obstetricians and Gynecologists, 21 December 2016.

As the days go on, the bleeding should settle: 'Primary postpartum haemorrhage (PPH)', Queensland Health, 1 August 2024.

Chapter 5: The (very) early days

It is definitely up to you as the parent to do your research, but knowing that it could potentially reduce the risk of SIDS (sudden infant death syndrome) made me feel a lot more comfortable with my decision to introduce the dummy: 'Information statement: Safe sleep: Using a dummy or pacifier', Red Nose, May 2021.

Without adequate vitamin K in the baby's body they can develop a rare disorder called vitamin K deficiency bleeding, which can ultimately lead to death: 'Tests and medicines for newborn babies', Royal Women's Hospital, n.d.

I can't stress enough the importance of checking in with your GP or care provider: 'Baby blues', Royal Women's Hospital, n.d.

Notes

Chapter 6: Home time – the first week

In terms of actual caffeine intake, our babies take in approximately 1 per cent of our caffeine intake, and it peaks in breastmilk an hour after consumption: 'Caffeine and breastfeeding', Australian Breastfeeding Association, April 2022.

I survived this period with plenty of baby wearing, arvo walks with bub in the pram and a lot of breastfeeding while binge-watching TV: 'Crying and unsettled babies – colic', Royal Children's Hospital Melbourne, March 2018.

Rest assured, not every baby will require medication and most outgrow it by the age of one; however, this definitely needs a medical diagnosis: 'Reflux (GOR) and GORD', Royal Children's Hospital Melbourne, May 2018.

The good news is most babies will outgrow CMPI as they enter their toddler/preschool years: 'Allergy and immunology', Royal Children's Hospital Melbourne, 22 December 2016.

Evening – these periods of crying are more common in the evening but can happen at any time of the day: 'Settling a crying baby', Sydney Children's Hospitals Network, 28 August 2024.

Another common cause of mastitis is the inability to drain breastmilk adequately, causing inflammation and/or blocked ducts: 'Mastitis', Royal Women's Hospital, n.d.

Chapter 7: The days are long but the years are short – the first month

Chances are you are simply one of the 50 per cent of mothers experiencing them, according to the Centre of Perinatal Excellence: 'Intrusive thoughts and perinatal OCD', Centre of Perinatal Excellence, n.d.

The Fourth Trimester

Chapter 8: Survival mode – the first three months

There is no doubt about it that intense exercise should take a back seat for the initial twelve weeks or so postpartum; however, this is always up to your own discretion: Inge, Philippa, Jessica J. Orchard, John W. Orchard, Rosie Purdue, 'Exercise after pregnancy', *Australian Journal of General Practice*, vol. 51, no. 3, March 2022.

Chapter 9: Sleep and settling

Instead of spending the majority of their sleep cycle in REM and non-REM sleep, they all of a sudden mimic an adult's sleep cycle of four stages (hello, four-month regression incoming): Pacheco, Danielle, Dr Abhinav Singh, 'How your baby's sleep cycle differs from your own', Sleep Foundation, 26 April 2023.

Acknowledgements

There are so many people to thank when it comes to me completing this book.

First and foremost, my local coffee shop, for allowing me to hog a table for hours on end several mornings a week for most of the year. For their endless smashed avocado and pots of English breakfast tea. God knows I wouldn't have been able to get through hours of typing without caffeine, my heart racing out of my chest and a good serve of protein. They made a lot of money in the till off me this year and they gave back a big wad of calories that's stacked on my hips, but I'm forever grateful for their wonderful thinking-and-writing space.

My partner, Ambrose. My stallion of a baby daddy who for the first time ever took the reins of being the 'stay at home parent' whilst I dashed off early in the morning to empty my brain. He did a damn good job of entertaining Scouty bum whilst Coco was at childcare and the older two were at school. He can do everything, that guy, except breastfeed Scouty of course, but honestly, nothing ever fazes him or stresses him out when it comes to the kids. Whingeing baby? No big deal, he goes for a walk with the pram. Bored baby? He goes for lunch with the babe. Tired baby? Straight to bed, snug and warm, with a delicious meal awaiting her when she wakes. The fun dad. The cool parent. The relaxed one. The patient one. My biggest cheerleader. Teaching me to 'roll with the punches' and 'just get through it, babe' . . . and that I did.

My kids. Gee whiz. Their patience. For letting me sit beside them, eyes glued to my screen, to finish 'just one more sentence' before giving them my full attention. For allowing me to duck off for an hour or two so I could concentrate and write some more. For screaming with excitement when they saw my book cover and saying, 'Wow, Mum, it says your name' . . . for being my number one supporters. 'I told my class you are famous, Mum' . . . bless them. 'Will you be as big as Taylor Swift?' they asked. Hopefully one day, I told them. Without my four babies there would be no passion for the fourth trimester. Forever indebted to

Acknowledgements

each of them for making that period so damn lovely. Tiring, but wonderful.

My mumma ... for proofreading my words with her blue biro and giving feedback as necessary. 'Are you sure you are allowed to do all this swearing, Amelia?' For always reminding me that my dad would have been so proud, as would my journalist grandfather. For always reminding me the clock was ticking and to stop procrastinating and just empty my head on paper. For handing me cups of tea whilst I sat on her couch writing away and distracting myself with too many social media breaks.

My siblings. Boy did they know how to push me. In particular, my sisters, Hannah and Georgia, for always breathing their anxiety on me to hurry up and just finish it. 'Are you seriously not done yet?' was the most common text message I received. They were SO encouraging and supportive of me that before I had Scout they sent me to Queensland with Ambrose to lock myself in a hotel room for a few nights whilst they watched the kids so I could finally spit some words out on paper. They really are so damn supportive.

My forever bestie, Cassie, who also doubles as my PA and admin manager these days. For hounding me ever so gently with her morning to-do texts, with my book ALWAYS at the top of the priority list. For bringing me salad rolls and cans of Coke and doughnuts and lollies and chocolate to keep me buzzing, and for always, without question, scooping my kids up and entertaining them whenever I had a deadline to meet. Nothing is ever too hard or overwhelming for her.

My obstetrician and good friend Dr Israelsohn. For always answering my text messages if I needed clarification on something and, more importantly, safely delivering my babies whilst keeping me in good health so I can be here today to spruik the importance of the fourth trimester.

To my followers and patients ... *woweeeeee* I feel like I owe all of this to so many of you. Your constant messages of support and desperate messages for help in the fourth trimester really gave me the push to write about something I feel so passionately about. All I ever want to do is help gorgeous mums and dads like you navigate the fourth trimester with ease and happiness.

To Penguin Books. For trusting me to write from the heart to every parent in this world. Never have I ever worked with a more patient, encouraging and supportive team. Your warmth towards me and your belief in my writing has been nothing short of beautiful.

Lastly, something I really want to reiterate now you've delved into my book. I am not a doctor (I wish) ... all of my words are written by me as a mumma of four. Do not take what I say as diagnostic – perhaps take it as your very own fourth trimester baby

Acknowledgements

bible. I am also a registered midwife, an International Board Certified Lactation Consultant (IBCLC) and a certified sleep consultant, so I really feel my personal experience can help shed some light on what to expect in the weeks ahead.

Whilst this book may assume the majority of mothers are in a relationship, more than 10 per cent of mothers in Australia are solo parents, whether by choice or by accident. I would like to add that many patients I have cared for during my ten years as a midwife have been on this journey by themselves, which just reinforces the need for more support in the fourth trimester. Whether you're single or in a relationship, co-parenting or coexisting, I hope you have found my book beneficial. What super parents you are. Just remember . . . whilst you are up feeding your baby overnight, so are a million other parents. You are never alone and I hope my book reminds you of this.

Thank you from the bottom of my heart. For even opening this book and for trusting my words of wisdom. Think of this book as a big warm hug from me to you.

Please do let me know if you enjoyed it and took solace from it.

Big love and in it together mumma,
Amelia X

Index

advice
  relatives, from 229–30
  unsolicited 180, 207, 230
allergies 156–8
anaemia 214
anxiety 137, 191, 193, 218, 227, 230
  daily walking 177
  motherhood, affecting 220–3
  postnatal *see* postnatal anxiety
Apgar score 47
appetite 233–4
Australian Institute of Health and Welfare 28
awake time 246–7, 258

babies
  awake time 246, 258
  differences between 79
  feed, play, sleep pattern 247
  first moment alone with 81–2
  first night 93–6
  first solo outing with 171
  first week at home 146
  first weigh 80–1
  head circumference 81
  length 81
  observations after birth 43

  overheating 85
  reflexes, checking 152
  six-week check-up 215
  skin 88
  sleep cycles 249
  temperature of 206–8
  tired signs 246
  unwell 45
  very early days 121–39
baby blues 17, 136–9
baby carrier 235
baby products
  monitors 193–5
  must-haves 144–6
bassinets
  choosing 145
  hats and 85
bath
  baby's first bath 88–9
  night routine, in 118
birth 27
  a long time conceiving, after 203
  birth experience 6–10
  difficult or complicated 38
  first 24 hours following 71–96
  hours following 30–1, 51–2
  people at 122

birth (*continued*)
  public system, in 30–1
  second 95
  vaginal 28–9, 55–8
birth trauma 37–41
birthing team
  midwife 41–4
  obstetrician 44–5
  paediatrician 45–7
  physiotherapist 47–50
bleeding
  blood in stools 158
  postpartum 22, 56, 61–2
  six weeks after birth 215
body
  being comfortable in own skin 230–1
  not rushing to get body back 180
  post-partum 231–3
  stretchmarks 231
bottle-feeding *see also* formula/bottle feeds
  long sleep blocks and 117–20
  mummas 112–14
  reasons for 113
bouncers 146
bowels
  opening 92–3
  stool softeners 92
breast(s)
  care of 107–10
  engorgement 101, 105, 109
  pain 109
breast pumps 99
breastfeeding
  amount of milk 77–8
  benefits of 103, 112
  breast is best 97
  caffeine and 148
  challenges 110–12
  cluster feeding 126–9, 254
  declining rates of 218
  education about 76
  first breastfeed 55, 71, 73–9
  first week at home 160–6

hydration 233
key to 105
latching on 65, 78, 108–9, 110, 160–1
learned skill, as 160
length of 163, 247
midwives assisting 108
night two 126–7, 253–5
oxytocin 67
skin-to-skin 55–6, 60
unswaddling during 85
women opting against 76, 97
breastmilk
  colostrum 75, 78, 100–1, 129
  'coming in' 102, 104, 107, 109, 136
  foremilk 102
  hindmilk 102
  mature milk 102–4
  stages of 99–100
  transitional milk 101–2
breech presentation 47

caesarean sections 28, 31–5
  delayed cord clamping 53
  emergency 29
  paediatricians 46
  recovering from 151
  six-week check-up 214
  skin-to-skin 58–60
  wound, closing 64
caffeine
  breastfeeding and 148
  capsules 145
  driving home from hospital 142
catheters 30
catnapping 260–3
centiles 81
cervix 215
childcare 242
China 267
  Golden Month 268
circadian rhythm 252
cleaners 181
colicky/reflux babies 22, 24, 130, 155–6, 258

Index

colostrum 75, 78, 100–1, 129
constipation 93
contraception 214, 217
cord blood, banking 53
cord clamping, delayed 52
cortisol 161
   skin-to-skin reducing 56
Cosy Nips 108
cots 145
   transitioning to 266
couples counselling 197–8
cow's milk protein intolerance 156, 158
crying 68–70
   colic, due to 155
   purple crying 158–9
   witching hour 156, 234–6

depression 137, 191, 218
   daily walking 177
   postnatal *see* postnatal depression
diabetes 214
doubts 202–3
doulas, postpartum 273
dressing baby
   post-birth 84–5
dummies 79, 127, 129–31, 142, 253

eating
   healthily 179
emergency
   caesarean sections 29
   home births, during 36–7
episiotomy 29, 40, 62, 92, 93
exercise 228–9
   intense 228
   light 227
   postpartum 151, 212, 228
   regime, resuming 228

feeding
   breastfeeding *see* breastfeeding
   feeding plan 80
   methods of 97
   night feeds 187

   partners helping with 187
   formula/bottle feeds 99
   babies refusing 113–14
   bottle-feeding *see* bottle-feeding
   equipment 77
   hospital regulations about 77
   stigma about 75, 113
   top-up feeds 75, 113, 118
four-month regression 265
fourth trimester
   being 'old hand' at 182
   challenges in 1, 209–10
   end of 265
   first baby 175
   first three months 209
   'firsts' following 276–7
   goal during 210
   loneliness during 189
   other countries, in 267
   period of grace, bonding and gratitude 274
   priorities during 210
   recharging in 176
   suggestions for 212
   surviving 210–13, 242
friends, talking to 177, 204–6, 225–7
fundal check 94

gastro-oesophageal reflux disease (GORD) 156
gestational diabetes 46, 75, 252
groundhog day 224–7

haemorrhaging postpartum 67
haemorrhoids 92
hair
   getting hair done 213
   loss, postpartum 223–4
hats
   safe sleeping 85
hearing test 133–5
help and support 222–3
   other countries, in 273
hepatitis B 132
home birth 35–7

honesty
  importance of 179
hospital
  amount of time in 218
  leaving 141–4
  use of time in 123
  visitors 122–4
  week in, post birth 222
hydration 177–9, 233
  breastfeeding and 233
  hair loss and 223

immunisations 131–6, 264
India 267
  Ayurvedic medicine 268–9
  jaappa 268
infertility 203
Instagram 148, 191
intimacy 217
intolerances/allergies 156–8
intrusive thoughts 191–2
intuition, trusting 180
involution 66
iron deficiency 214

jaundice testing 134, 152
kids
  helping to care for 182
  managing, with a newborn 183–5

labour, induction 29
lactation consultants 109–10, 112, 117, 166
lactose intolerance 156
Latin America
  la cuarentena 269
laxatives 93, 100
lochia 61
loneliness 189–91, 209
lullabies 259

Malaysia
  pantang 271
mastitis 109–10, 115, 165
Maternal and Child Health

nurse 112, 149, 152–5, 189
  mental health issues 218
  role 152
maternal instincts 10
maternity leave 220, 222, 237, 238–41
  paid 241
meals 233–4
meconium 89–92, 100
melatonin 21, 252, 259
mental health 217–23
  fathers, problems experienced by 199
  issues 138, 223
  prioritising 179
  stigma around 218
  walking and 229
midwife
  birthing team, in 41–4
  breastfeeding, assisting 108
  buzzing 82
  first 24 hours, in 71–2
  home births, assisting 36
  meaning of 41
  settling babies 129
milk ejection reflex 65, 116
monitor-checking
  obsessions with 193
motherhood
  anxiety and 220–3
  being housebound 227–8
  consensus about 274–5
  feelings about newborn period 243
  home, spending time at 224, 227
  isolation at home 224
  loneliness 189–91, 209
  realities of 274
  time passing quickly 243
mothers' group 206
'mum intuition' 229

nannies 242
nappies
  changes 91
  fathers changing 200

Index

first nappy 84
nappy bag 145
neonatal intensive care unit 46, 125–6
  expressing milk 125
  nurses and midwives in 125
The Netherlands
  kraamzorg 271–2
newborn hearing screen 133–4
newborn screen test 133
Nigeria
  omugwo 272
nights
  dream feed 202
  feeds 187
  night routine, setting 118
  night two 126–9
nipples
  damage to 107, 115
  nipple shields 99
  pain 107, 109
  tender 107
'no', saying 181
nourishment
  postpartum 233–4, 269

obsessive compulsive disorder 191
obstetrician
  birthing team, in 44–5
  six-week check-up 44, 213–15
outing
  first, with bub 171
  packing for 173
overfeeding 69
oxytocin 15, 56, 65–7, 200

paediatrician
  birthing team, in 45–7
  six-week check-up 215
pain
  birth, following 65–7
  breast pain 109
  cramps 67
  nipple pain 107, 109
partners

bonding with baby 200
booking date with 180
checking in with 198
dealing with 195–8
debriefing 199
first few weeks, during 149
helping 200
postnatal mental health problems 199
prioritising 217
relationship changes 195–8
returning to work 168–71
pelvic floor 181, 215
  exercises 49
  healing 228
  lifting and 151
physiotherapist
  birthing team, in 47–50
  women's health physio 228
placenta
  birthing 67
  delivery of 56
  retained 62
poo
  baby's first poo 58, 89
  meconium 89–92, 100
  mother's first poo 92–3
postnatal anxiety 137, 176, 218, 221
  fathers, in 199
  increasing rates of 218
  sleep deprivation and 223
postnatal depression 137, 176, 218
  fathers, in 199
  increasing rates of 218
  sleep deprivation and 223
post-traumatic stress disorder 40
prams 144–5
pregnancy
  complications 29
prolapse 49
pumping 114–17
  benefits 115
  breast pumps 99
  tips for 115–16

purple crying 158–9

rape 76
Red Nose guidelines 251, 266
reflux 156
resuscitation cot 57, 59
routines 25, 249–51

safe sleeping 85, 152, 193, 251–2
   Red Nose guidelines 251, 266
serum bilirubin level blood test 134
sex
   birth, following 215
   kids, after 216
   postpartum 216
   six-week period 215, 261
sexual harassment 76
sexual relationship
   factors influencing 217
shopping online 212
shoulder dystocia delivery 40
shower 237
   daily 212
   first, after giving birth 85–8
   phantom shower cries 192–3
SIDS 131, 251–2, 280
six-week
   check-up 44, 213–15, 261
   milestone 261
skin-to-skin
   birth, from 105
   breastfeeding 55–6, 60
   caesarean birth 58–60
   special care nursery, babies in 56, 125
   vaginal birth 55–8
sleep
   babies 70, 220, 249
   baby sleep cycles 249
   birth, from 105
   bottle-feeding and 117–20
   broken 185–9
   catnapping 261–2
   co-sleeping 245
   dark room, in 258–9

   four-month regression 265
   going to bed early 179, 212
   good quality,
      restorative 70 newborns 245
   importance of 5
   night 1 252
   night 2 253–5
   night 3 256
   nights 4-7 256
   safe sleeping 85, 152, 193, 251–2
   'sleeping through' 118
   week 2 256–7
   week 3 257–8
   week 4 260
   week 5 260
   week 6 261
   weeks 6-12 264
sleep consultant 5, 162, 246, 250
sleep deprivation
   mental health issues and 223
   preparing for 118–19
   tapping out 236
   two days of 129
   two young children, with 221
sleep school 220–1
sleeping bags 265–6
social life
   post-baby 204–5
social media 78, 144, 167, 261
special care nursery 46
   skin-to-skin in 56, 125
startle reflex 246
stitches 62–3
streaming services 237–8
stress, modern 218
sudden infant death syndrome
   (SIDS) 131, 251–2, 280
swaddling 246

tapping out 236–7
thyroid 214

umbilical cord
   button, checking 152
   delayed clamping 52

Index

urination
　baby urinating 91
uterus 214–15
　contracting 57, 66–7, 75, 181
　fundal check 94
　pains post birth 65–7
　postpartum bleeding 61–2

vaccinations
　first, after birth 59
　second round of 171
vacuum delivery 47, 69, 94, 151
vagina
　post-birth check 94
　recovering 215
vaginal birth 28–9
　recovering from 151
　skin-to-skin 55–8
visitors
　at home 18, 166–8
　choosing 212
　hospital 122–4
　limiting 177

vitamins
　hair loss and 223
　vitamin D 149, 177, 184, 212, 227, 229
　vitamin K 59, 132

walking, daily 177, 212, 227, 228–9, 237
weaning 79
weighing
　first months of life, in 80
　first weigh 80–1
weighing(*continued*)
　health nurses, by 153
weight
　birth weight, regaining 80, 154
　losing, after birth 80, 107
white noise 259
witching hour 156, 234–6
work
　partner returning to 168
　returning to 239, 241–2
worthless, feeling 228

Powered by Penguin

Looking for more great reads, exclusive content and book giveaways?
Subscribe to our weekly newsletter.

Scan the QR code or visit penguin.com.au/signup